JESU

BROKEN
CHURCH

Reimagining Our Sunday Traditions

from a New Testament Perspective

PETER DEHAAN, PHD

ISBNs:
>   978-1-948082-47-1 (e-book)
>   978-1-948082-48-8 (paperback)
>   978-1-948082-49-5 (hardcover)
>   978-1-948082-56-3 (audiobook)

Published by Spiritually Speaking Publishing

Credits:
>   Developmental editor: Kathryn Wilmotte
>   Copy editor/proofreader: Robyn Mulder
>   Cover design: Cassia Friello
>   Author photo: Chele Reagh, PippinReaghDesign

To all who sense that something is missing

Peter DeHaan's Books

For a complete, up-to-date list of all Peter's books, go to PeterDeHaan.com/books.

Dear Theophilus series:

- *Dear Theophilus: A 40-Day Devotional Exploring the Life of Jesus through the Gospel of Luke*

- *Dear Theophilus Acts: 40 Devotional Insights for Today's Church*

- *Dear Theophilus Isaiah: 40 Prophetic Insights about Jesus, Justice, and Gentiles*

- *Dear Theophilus Minor Prophets: 40 Prophetic Teachings about Unfaithfulness, Punishment, and Hope*

- *Dear Theophilus Job: 40 Insights About Moving from Despair to Deliverance*

- *Dear Theophilus John's Gospel: 40 Reflections about Jesus's Life and Love*

52 Churches series:

- *52 Churches: A Yearlong Journey Encountering God, His Church, and Our Common Faith*

- *The 52 Churches Workbook: Become a Church that Matters*

- *More Than 52 Churches: The Journey Continues*

- *The More Than 52 Churches Workbook: Pursue Christian Community and Grow in Our Faith*

Bible Bios series:

- *Women of the Bible: The Victorious, the Victims, the Virtuous, and the Vicious*

- *Friends and Foes of Jesus: Explore How People in the New Testament React to God's Good News*

Other books:

- *Woodpecker Wars: Celebrating the Spirituality of Everyday Life*

- *95 Tweets: Celebrating Martin Luther in the 21st Century*

- *How Big is Your Tent? A Call for Christian Unity, Tolerance, and Love*

Be the first to hear about Peter's new books and receive updates when you sign up at www.PeterDeHaan.com/updates.

Contents

Zealous about Church

"**W**hy do you so hate the church?"

Shocked, I furrow my eyebrows and scowl at my friend. "I don't hate church."

"But you're always criticizing it in your blog."

This gives me pause. True, much of my writing about the church doesn't celebrate what she does well but rebukes her for what she does poorly or doesn't do at all.

"I don't hate the church," I say again, as if trying to convince myself. "I love the church, really I do. I write to challenge her to do better because I know she can."

My friend nods, but I'm not sure I convince her.

In truth, I'm zealous about church.

Over the centuries the church has done much to advance the cause of Jesus, help people find their way to eternal life, and perform acts of generosity that point an unbelieving world to Jesus. Today's church continues to do that. And I hope church has done that for you.

But lest we feel smug about the church's achievements, today's church does only a small fraction of what she could be doing, of what she should be doing. I'm sad to say that the church has lost her way. She's off track and has missed the mark for much of her existence. This pains me as much as a spike driven into my heart, into my very soul, the core of my being. I mourn what the church is because she's falling far short of her potential, of her calling.

It's like being a parent of a brilliant, gifted child who muddles her way through school and gets Cs, even though she could be earning As in advanced classes. As a loving parent, we'd do whatever we could to shake the apathetic inertia out of our child and get her to live up to her potential. But since she won't, we prod her to do better.

Just as we would do this for our children, I do this for my church with the same imperative passion. I metaphorically shake her in hopes that she'll do better—because she can. I do this through the words I write. It's the best way I know to help.

At this point, some of you may be saying "Amen, preach it!" but others—most of you, I suspect—may have felt your hackles rise at my insulting, impertinent words. You're angry and thinking about slamming this book shut. You might be yelling at me right now. That's okay. I get it. But before you bail on me, I challenge you to stick with me a little bit longer. Give me a chance to explain.

A Biblical Church

If asked, most people would say the practices of their church are biblical. I'd say that about every church I've been part of. I'd even say this for every church I visited in my book *52 Churches* and its sequels.

Let's run through a typical church service.

There's preaching. That's in the Bible. Check.

There's singing. Also in the Bible. Check.

There's praying, an offering (or two), and a concluding blessing. All biblical. Check, check, check.

We meet every Sunday, just like the Bible says. Check. (More on that later.) We may volunteer, tithe, and respect our pastor. More checkmarks. Yes, today's church services are most biblical—or so they seem.

Yet, we read the Bible through the lens of our experiences. The things we do in church, we find mentioned in the Bible. This confirms we're doing things the biblical way, God's way. Yet we may be connecting dots we shouldn't connect.

For example, the Bible tells us to not give up meeting together (Hebrews 10:24–25). Is this a command to go to church every Sunday? Not really—despite what many preachers claim.

We take our experiences, then we find justification for them in the Bible, even if it isn't what Scripture says. This is confirmation bias. We do it all the time. You, me, everyone. But we must stop.

Sunday Church

Most Christians have a practice of going to church on Sunday. Some people even go twice. Why do we do that? Why Sunday?

The quick answer most people would give is that that's what the Bible says to do. But I don't see that in Scripture. Yes, it does say that we should not give up meeting together (Hebrews 10:25), but it says nothing about church or Sunday. It just says to pursue spiritual community.

Why Sunday? It's always perplexed me why we meet on Sunday and not Saturday. Granted, Jesus rose from the dead on the first day of the week, on Sunday. And his followers happened to be together on that day, but they were hiding out of fear, lest they too be captured and crucified (John 20:19).

And Paul did tell the people in Corinth to set money aside on the first day of each week for a special collection for the people in Jerusalem (1 Corinthians 16:2). But this was a command to one church for a short-term initiative.

When it comes to Sunday, that's about it. The word Sunday doesn't appear in the Bible. So meeting on Sunday seems to be more of a tradition than anything else. I certainly don't see this commanded in Scripture.

What About the Sabbath? The word Sabbath occurs 150 times in the Old Testament. God gives a lot of instructions about the Sabbath. Two key commands reoccur.

First, the Sabbath is a day of rest (Deuteronomy 5:14 and about fifteen more places). God tells his people to do no work on the Sabbath. The other six days of the week are for work and the seventh, the Sabbath, our Saturday, is for rest.

This is what God did when he created us. Six days of work followed by a day of rest. There's a nice rhythm to this. Work and then rest. Our rest on the seventh day gives us a break from our labors. This prepares us to function more effectively for the next six days.

The second key element of the Sabbath is that it's holy (Exodus 20:8 and about twenty more places). The Sabbath is set apart. The Bible also says to execute anyone desecrating the Sabbath (Exodus 31:14). That's some serious stuff.

But what does it mean to keep the Sabbath holy? Though we can find some guidelines in Scripture, it's up to us to determine what this means for us today and how to apply it.

Here are some secondary verses about the Sabbath.

- Observing and celebrating the Sabbath is a lasting covenant (Exodus 31:16).
- The Sabbath is a sign between God and his people (Ezekiel 20:12, 20).

- Every Sabbath requires a burnt offering (Numbers 28:10).
- We should delight in the Sabbath (Isaiah 58:13).

Yet to Isaiah, God also says, "I cannot bear your worthless assemblies." This includes their Sabbaths (Isaiah 1:13). And in Hosea, God says he will stop the Sabbath celebrations (Hosea 2:11). This certainly gives us something to contemplate.

What Should We Do? Interestingly, just as I've found no command in the New Testament to meet every Sunday, I've yet to find a verse in the Old Testament that says to meet every Sabbath. Though some of the Old Testament's celebrations did fall on the Sabbath, which required the people to have special observances on those days, this wasn't a weekly occurrence.

If we're going to do things according to the Bible, the one essential command is that we must not give up meeting together. This doesn't necessarily mean church, Sunday, or weekly. It simply means pursuing intentional spiritual community. Though Sunday church may be one way to accomplish this, it's not necessarily the best way.

Next, if we want to factor the Old Testament into our thinking, we should set aside one day for rest and keep it holy. That's about it. How we do this seems up to us.

Meeting Together

Back to Hebrews 10:25. This passage doesn't mention church. It says "meeting together," that is, spending time with each other. If you came to my house—which would be far more personal than reading this book—we'd be meeting together, just as the Bible commands.

If we go out to eat each Sunday, that's meeting together. If we do game night once a month, that's meeting together. So would having a movie night, hanging out at the coffee shop, and working together on a service project. These are all examples of us meeting together. Going to church is just one possibility. But let's remember, this passage doesn't command us to go to church. It merely tells us to meet. How we meet is up to us to determine. Sort of. (Again, more on that later.)

However—here I go ruffling your feathers again—going to one of today's churches on Sunday morning may be one of the least significant ways we can meet. At most churches today, we spend the better part of an hour twisting our neck to see around the back of someone's head as others entertain us. Yes, today's church is more about a chosen few performing than about the majority present taking part.

Then we go home. This is scarcely a prime example of meeting together. If our church service—even the best ones I've ever been to—is us meeting together as the Bible commands, we're doing a poor job of it. We're getting Cs (or Ds or even Fs) when we should be getting As in advanced classes.

That's why I mourn for the church I love so much. That's why I write. I write because I know she's capable of so much more.

I know this is a lot to take in.

Take a deep breath with me, and then let's turn the page together. We have much to cover.

When I criticize the church, it's because I love her and want her to do better.

Questions: Are you zealous about church? Why or why not? What would you like to see changed at your church? All churches?

Chapter 1:

The Old Testament Approach

To understand where we are now, we need to go back and look at where we began. We need to start our investigation in the Old Testament.

Once, when leading a Bible study, I asked our group to turn to an Old Testament passage.

Our newest member glared at me. "We're Christians. Why are we looking at the Old Testament?"

I raise an eyebrow. "The Old Testament is relevant to us too."

"But Jesus fulfilled the Old Testament, so it no longer applies."

"Yet the Bible says *all* Scripture comes from God and is useful for teaching" (2 Timothy 3:16). My friend gave me a weak nod and turned to the passage without further complaint. Our group ended up having an insightful, faith-building discussion. I hope that will happen again with us now.

In the Old Testament, when God gives Moses the Law, he sets three key expectations for worship, along with a lengthy set of mind-numbing details to guide the practices he wants his people to follow. God addresses this throughout Exodus, Leviticus, Numbers, and Deuteronomy.

These three main elements relate to the worship space, the worship team, and their financial support: tithes and offerings. The rest of God's instructions support these three tenets indirectly by guiding the people into right living as a daily way of worshiping God through their personal practices and interpersonal interactions. These prepare them to move into relationship with him and worship him more fully through their many annual feasts, festivals, and celebrations.

A Place

In the Old Testament, God is most particular about the place where his people are to worship him. He gives detailed instructions on how they are to do it.

First, God sets specific parameters for the tabernacle and surrounding worship space. He gives exact instructions for its size, materials, and construction methods. In some cases, he even specifies who is to oversee the work (see Exodus 26–27 and 35–36).

The tabernacle and adjacent area function as a home for the various objects used in the people's religious practices. God gives detailed directions for these implements of worship too. He specifies dimensions, base components, and fabrication instructions. Again, he sometimes names who is to head up the production (see Exodus 28–31, 33–34, and 37–40).

Later the people get situated in the land God promised for them. In doing so they transition from a roaming people to a nation with borders. They no longer need a portable tabernacle that they can set up and tear down as they roam about the desert.

Years later King David has the idea to build a temple to honor God. Although prohibited from erecting this grand edifice himself—because he was a warring military leader with blood on his hands—the king sets aside provisions for its construction (2 Samuel 7:1–17).

It's David's son Solomon who builds this permanent worship space for God's people (1 Kings 6). In doing so, the tabernacle built by Moses transitions to the temple built by Solomon. The portable tabernacle of the desert as the focal point of worship shifts to the permanent temple in Jerusalem.

With few exceptions, the people must go to this house of worship, the tabernacle—and later the temple—to approach the Almighty. God's people see the tabernacle/temple as his dwelling place here on earth (1 Kings 8:13). They must go there to experience a divine encounter with him.

Clergy

But the people won't connect with God directly. They refuse. They're afraid of him. Here's what happened.

In the Old Testament we see Moses on Mount Sinai, hanging out with God. They're having a spiritual confab of the highest order. God has some words—many words, in fact—for Moses to give to the people. In one instance God says they will serve as his kingdom of priests, a holy nation (Exodus 19:6). Did you catch that?

God intends to have a whole nation of priests. And who will they be priests to? Implicitly, other nations, the rest of the world. But this doesn't occur. I've found no evidence in the Bible of them as a nation ever serving as priests. What happened?

Just one chapter later in the book of Exodus, the people see a display of God's awe-inspiring might. They pull back in terror. They keep their distance. God's magnificent display of power terrifies them. The people are afraid of the Almighty.

Because of their intense fear, they don't want to hear what he has to say. Instead, they beg Moses to function as their intermediary. They ask their leader to do what they're afraid of doing: listen to God. Moses serves as their first liaison with their Creator (Exodus 20:18–21). In effect, this makes Moses the people's first priest, though the duty officially goes to his brother, Aaron. In doing so, the people fail to become God's nation of priests.

After this, God seems to switch to plan B.

Instead of his people being a kingdom of priests, he sets some of them aside—descendants of Aaron— to serve as ministers, functioning as the middlemen between the people and God. This is something far different than his original desire for everyone to be a priest and connect with him directly.

This idea of divine-human interaction isn't something new. Recall that God talks with Adam in the Garden of Eden (Genesis 3:8–10). And after sin forces Adam and Eve's exile from their paradise, God speaks directly to Cain, confronting him after the murder of his brother, Abel (Genesis 4:8–10). Then once sin fills the world with evil, God approaches Noah with a solution (Genesis 6:11–22). Much later God has multiple interactions with Abraham (such as in Genesis 17:9), as well as his wife Sarah (Genesis 18:10–15). God then meets Moses through the burning bush (Exodus 3) and later talks with him face to face (Exodus 33:11). And God also speaks to other people in this time between Adam and Moses.

This shows a consistent history of direct communication between God and his people. Now he wants to talk to his chosen tribe, but they're afraid of him and don't want to hear his words directly (Exodus 20:18–21).

They demand an intermediary, someone to reveal the Almighty to them. They want an ambassador to represent God to them. To address this, God sets up the priesthood. These priests will serve him in his temple and be his representatives to his chosen ones. They'll serve as the liaison between God and his people, just as they requested.

Though this begins with Moses, the religious infrastructure God sets up requires a large team. We have the priests: Aaron and his descendants (who are Levites). And the rest of the tribe of Levi plays a supporting role in God's plan to connect with his people.

Finances

This religious structure is vast. The priests lead the people in their worship of the Almighty God, and the entire Levite tribe supports this effort. Accomplishing this requires support. To address this, God institutes a temple tax of sorts: the annual tithe (Numbers 18:21). This is a mandated obligation to give 10 percent to support the maintenance of the tabernacle and the needs of the staff.

But it's not just one annual tithe. There's a second one too (Deuteronomy 14:22–27). In addition, a third tithe for the poor occurs every three years (Deuteronomy 14:28–29). This means that each year God's people give between 20 and 30 percent to him in support of the tabernacle/temple, the people who work there, and those in need. It averages out to 23.3%, approaching one quarter.

Take a moment to imagine giving one fourth to God.

In addition to the mandated tithes are various required offerings and sacrifices that relate to annual events (such as in Exodus 12 and Exodus 30:10). God commands his people to adhere to all these obligations. On top of these are voluntary offerings and gifts (such as in Leviticus 22:21). God expects a lot from them financially.

The Old Testament religious institution is expensive to sustain. And God expects each one of his people to do their part.

The Old Testament Model for Church

This is the Old Testament model for church: a place (tabernacle and then temple), clergy and support staff (priests and Levites), and financial support (tithes and offerings). We still follow this model today.

In the Old Testament, God established the tabernacle/ temple as the place for his people to go to meet him. He set up the priests as professional clergy to be his liaison to his chosen ones. And he instituted tithes and offerings to finance the whole thing.

Questions: How do modern churches tend to mirror the three key Old Testament elements that God ordained for his people's religious practices? What roles do location, paid staff, and offerings play in our church today?

Chapter 2:

Following the Old Testament Model

Our churches today function in much the same way as in the Old Testament—even though Jesus came to fulfill the Old Testament laws and prophets (Matthew 5:17). We pursue these same three key elements. We meet in a building, hire paid staff to represent God to us, and have an ongoing need for money to keep the institution afloat and moving forward.

Building

I often hear the question, "Where do you go to church?" This is an inquiry about location. In standard usage, the word "church" refers to a place, not a people. It's a structure more so than the community that meets there.

This mindset is pervasive within the church and even more so for outsiders. In short, people go to a church building to experience God. The implication is that we can't connect with him at other locations or through different situations. We want a Sunday morning service in a church building.

We go to church. We connect with God. Then we head home. Once we leave the parking lot, we revert to non-church mode and resume our everyday life.

Most people, both those with a religious background and those without it, view a church without their own building as suspicious, as second-rate, somehow less than. Once, while doing street ministry, I met a man who admitted it would be good for him to go back to church. He asked where our church was. I told him we met in small groups in people's homes. He shook his head. "I want to go to a real church."

People assume—both those inside the church community and those outside it—that a church without a building will one day mature to a point where she can have her own place to meet. Then she will be a *real* church.

In addition, for many churchgoers, the thought of attending in a non-typical space is an anathema to having a true worship experience. They feel that to truly connect with God they must travel to a dedicated church building, usually on Sunday morning.

Staff

The second element of today's church is the staff. In most cases they are paid. Yes, sometimes volunteers help, donating many hours of their time each week, but despite their generosity most churches rely on paid employees to function.

For small churches, the paid staff is the pastor alone, while for larger congregations it's a pastoral team, made up of full-time and part-time paid personnel.

A church-growth expert once told me that a single pastor could sufficiently shepherd a congregation of up to 150 people. Beyond that level, the sole pastor required help to address the needs of the congregation and deal with the details brought on by this expanded scope. The specialist had a formula for that too: each additional one hundred people in the church required one more staff person. This formula seems to track at the various churches I've been part of over the years.

In the same way that most people expect to go to a dedicated worship space on Sunday, they carry expectations of the paid staff who work there, especially the minister. Just as the people in the Old Testament once lined up each day to see Moses, overburdening him and keeping him busy from sunup to sunset (Exodus 18:13), we tend to do the same to our clergy today.

Collectively we insist that our ministers be available for us whenever we need them. This includes a crisis, such as a death, health scare, financial need, lost job, or wayward child. We also want them there for our celebrations. This means our family births (baptisms, christenings, or dedications), our weddings (officiating), and even our milestone birthdays and anniversaries. We also presume their support for our own God-honoring initiatives. And we freely dump our burdens on them in the form of prayer requests. When we call, email, or text, we expect a quick response.

They're here to serve us. That's what we pay them for.

When they wisely refer us to another person who can help us, just as Moses's father-in-law recommended that he do (Exodus 18:21), we react with indignation. We withdraw our support for this leader we feel has slighted us (2 Corinthians 6:12). And we seldom do this silently, often resorting to gossip and even slander (3 John 1:9–11). Sometimes we launch a campaign to replace our once-esteemed leader. To add weight to our hurt, we may threaten to withhold our financial (and emotional) support of the church. And to our shame, we often follow through (Malachi 3:6–12).

Money

The third key element of today's church is financial support. She needs money to function, lots of it. We often refer to this need for money as tithes and offerings. Some leaders call for pledges and then urge people to meet their financial commitments each Sunday. Other churches levy assessments.

Over the years I've heard many ministers plead for money from their congregations, insisting that we must give 10 percent of our income to the local church. I'm not sure if they're merely parroting what they've heard others say, don't know their Scripture, or don't care, but the Bible never says to give 10 percent to the local church. Remember, the Old Testament tithe went to fuel the national religion.

In a typical church, most of the budget goes to cover facility costs and staffing. This often approaches 90 percent of the total budget and sometimes requires all of it, only to still fall short. This doesn't leave too much money—if any—for ministry and outreach.

But lest we complain about the size of our church's budget and our leader's calls for financial generosity, remember that this is our own doing. We've brought this upon ourselves. We expect to meet in our own dedicated worship space. And we hire staff to serve as our liaison between us and God. These things carry a price tag, and our church budget reflects it.

The Exceptions

Though it's true that some churches are exceptions to this—and take exception to what I've just written—they are the minority. To need less financial support usually stems from one of two factors. The first is having a non-typical meeting space. And the second is enjoying a lot of volunteers to do the work that normally falls to paid staff. In some cases, both elements are present, which allows for much more of the congregants' giving to go to ministry and outreach, instead of buildings and payroll.

This allows them to move from an inward focus to an outward emphasis. Every church should strive to move toward this outcome. The kingdom of God will advance more powerfully when we do.

Today we cling to the Old Testament model of church. We go to a church building to encounter God. We're led by professional clergy who represent him to us. And we give our tithes and offerings to pay for it all.

Questions: Would you ever consider meeting for church in a nontraditional space? Do you expect paid clergy to teach you about God? Why or why not?

Chapter 3:

Jesus Fulfills the Old Testament Practice

Today's church still follows the Old Testament model: we have a church building where we go to worship God, hire a minister who represents the Almighty to us, and take a collection to support the whole thing.

This is not what Jesus had in mind. Through his sacrificial death, in one single action, Jesus does away with the need to go to a building, hire staff, and take an offering. We should do the same.

This all hinges on Jesus.

Jesus draws people to him—both then and now. The words he speaks and the hope he communicates attract them. Two thousand years ago, people assume he came to replace the Old Testament Law and the work of the prophets, but this isn't his calling.

Jesus doesn't come to do away with what the Old Testament teaches. Instead, his mission is to bring the Old Testament into fruition, according to God's plan, set in place from the beginning. Jesus makes this clear. He says, "I have not come to abolish the Law and the prophets but to fulfill them" (Matthew 5:17).

How does Jesus do this?

Jesus Becomes the Ultimate Sacrifice

The Old Testament is packed with instructions for making sacrificial offerings, commands that show the people's relationship with God. These sacrifices have various meanings, but one key sacrifice occurs—and reoccurs—to remedy sin. An animal must die because the people have sinned. Since the people continue to sin, animal sacrifices persist as a requirement. These sin sacrifices must happen over and over, year after year, century after century.

Jesus, in his sacrificial death on the cross, becomes the ultimate sacrifice for sin to end all sin sacrifices. In his once-and-for-all sacrifice, he dies to make us right with God, to reconcile us into a right relationship with our Creator.

Jesus Turns Law into Love

Jesus reforms the conventional view of loving our neighbors and hating our enemies (Deuteronomy

23:6 and Psalm 139:21–22). Instead, he wants us to *love* our enemies and pray for them (Matthew 5:43–48).

Despite Jesus's fresh way of looking at the assumptions of his people, his disciples struggle to understand what he means. They grapple to reconcile his teachings with their traditions.

One such person asks Jesus to cite the greatest commandment in the Old Testament. Jesus's answer is love. He says to "love God with all your heart, soul, and mind." This stands as the greatest commandment, but then he adds one more. He says to "love others as much as you love yourself" (Matthew 22:36–40). These two simple principles—love God and love others—summarize the purpose and intent of the entire Old Testament Law and the writings of the prophets.

Jesus removes a set of impossible-to-please laws and replaces them with one principle: love.

Jesus Changes Our Perspectives

When we consider that Jesus came to fulfill the Law of Moses and the writings of the prophets, what's important to understand is that we must see these passages in their proper perspective. This doesn't mean to ignore what was because Jesus fulfills it. It means we should consider the Old Testament in its context, where people lived under the Law of Moses—not our present freedom through Jesus (John 8:36). In addition to teaching the people how to worship God and the right way to live, the Law and the prophets also point them to the coming Savior, Jesus.

In Genesis through Malachi, we see repeated allusions to Jesus and the freedom he plans to offer to us now. And if we read the Old Testament with care, we will also see that this future revelation about Jesus applies to all people, not just God's chosen tribe.

Yes, Jesus comes to fulfill the Law and the writings of the prophets. We're the benefactors of that. Now let's apply this to the Old Testament ideas of temple, priests, and tithes.

New Temple

When Jesus overcomes death, the curtain in the temple rips apart, exposing the inner sanctum of the most holy place (Matthew 27:51). This supernatural rending of the veil symbolically allows everyone direct access to God. No longer is God separated from his people, distant and removed (Hebrews 9:3–10 and Hebrews 10:19–25).

The Almighty is now approachable for everyone. God ceases living in the temple and begins living in us. Our bodies become the temple of God. No longer do we need a physical building. We are his temple.

Yet we cling to the Old Testament idea of a temple and forget how Jesus fulfills it. Jesus's disciple Peter helps us understand this. He writes that we are living stones built into a spiritual temple (1 Peter 2:5).

Yes, this verse is confounding.

It challenges our perspective of needing to go to church to experience God. Peter's words flip this practice on its head, and that's the point. Jesus turns the old ways upside down and makes something new. We must embrace this. We must change our perspective.

As living stones, we are alive—not inanimate rocks. Jesus may have this in mind in his rebuff of the Pharisees who take offense to the praise his followers offer. He tells the religious elite that if the crowd didn't celebrate his arrival, the stones would cry out to exalt him (Luke 19:37–40). To worship him, the rocks would have to come alive. In a sense they would need to be living stones.

As Jesus's living stones today, our actions matter. We live for Jesus. We exist to honor him, praise him, and glorify him. Our purpose is to tell others about him through our actions and—when needed—even through our words. Our faith is alive, and what we do must show it.

Back in chapter 1 we talked about King David sharing his idea with Nathan to build a temple to honor God. At first the prophet gives David approval, along with a blessing. But that night God appears to Nathan in a vision to give the prophet his perspective.

David, according to God, isn't the one to build God's temple. Instead, God will see to the temple construction *himself.* After David dies, one of his off-spring will succeed him. He is the one who will build a house for God. And God will establish his kingdom forever (2 Samuel 7:11–13).

Though Solomon, David's son, does indeed build a temple for God, Solomon isn't the one Nathan's vision speaks of. At that time, Solomon is already alive, whereas the vision states that God will raise up someone *after* David dies. This couldn't refer to Solomon.

Though David understands this prophecy to mean Solomon, it's a prophecy about Jesus. The fulfillment of Nathan's vision comes through Jesus when we, as his followers, collectively come together to build God's temple, his spiritual house, for us to worship him as his holy priests. Jesus, as *the* living Stone, takes us as *his* living stones and builds us into a spiritual house, a temple for God (1 Peter 2:4–10).

As living stones, we become part of the construction of God's new worship space. If we comprise his temple, we don't need to go to church to meet him. This is because, as his temple, he's already in our presence, and we're already in his. This means we can experience him at anytime, anywhere. Through Jesus, God's temple exists everywhere we go.

New Priests

After saying we're living rocks built into God's spiritual house, Peter adds two more mind-blowing thoughts. He says these first two truths—that we're breathing stones shoring up God's temple—set up two more spiritual concepts.

Through Jesus, we become a holy priesthood so that we can offer spiritual sacrifices to God (1 Peter 2:5). If we are truly priests through what Jesus did for us, then we don't need ministers to point us to God, explain him to us, or help us know him. God wants us to do that for ourselves as his holy priests.

Remember that back in Exodus, God calls his people to be a nation of priests (Exodus 19:6). But they recoil from that and refuse to cooperate. Later, Isaiah looks forward to the time when the children of God will become the Lord's priests, ministers of the Almighty (Isaiah 61:6).

At last, through Jesus we're poised to do just that. And Peter confirms this. As followers of Jesus—his disciples—we're a royal priesthood. This makes us his holy nation, an elite possession of God. Our purpose is to praise him for what he did when he saved us from the darkness of sin and moved us into the light of his love (1 Peter 2:9).

Though Jesus is the ultimate sin sacrifice to end all sacrifices, we honor what he did by living lives as holy priests that serve as an ongoing tribute to him. This spiritual sacrifice (see Romans 12:1) replaces the animal sacrifices we read about throughout the Old Testament.

This thinking is so countercultural to how most Christians live today that it bears careful contemplation. Through Jesus we can do things in a new way. We are living stones built into his spiritual temple, serving as a holy priesthood to offer him spiritual sacrifices (1 Peter 2:5). Read that again: We are living stones built into his spiritual temple, serving as a holy priesthood to offer him spiritual sacrifices.

Wow!

This can change everything—and it should.

No longer do priests (ministers) need to serve as our liaison between the Creator and the created. Instead, all who follow Jesus become his priests—a nation of priests—just as God wanted back in Exodus 19:6.

This means that the laity, serving as priests to each other, should minister to one another, not hire someone else to do it for them. No longer is there a need for paid staff to be the link between God and his people. Everyone can now approach God directly, hearing from him and acting on his behalf. The Holy Spirit whom Jesus sent to us sees to that—if we are but willing to listen, hear, and obey what he says.

New Finances

Last is that pesky temple tax, which we call a tithe. Today, the cost for a church's building and employees can make up 90 to 100 percent of its budget. I'll never forget my first time serving as a deacon and looking closely at our church budget. The numbers shocked me. Fifty-five percent went to staff expenses and 38 percent went to building-related costs. That left 7 percent for ministry, outreach, missions, and benevolence. For each hundred dollars I gave, only seven dollars went to help other people.

Over the years I've served on boards at four churches, three as a deacon and one as an elder. The budget for each one, whether small, large, or in between, followed similar percentages. At best, a mere 10 percent of the funds went for outreach and community needs. And when the need for budget cuts arose— which invariably occurred from time to time—expenses not related to staff and building were slashed first.

But once we remove the facility and the paid staff from the equation, there's no longer such a need for money. Does that mean we can forget about tithing?

Yes . . . and no.

The Bible talks a lot about tithing. In the Old Testament, God instituted tithes to support the religious structure he mandated for his people. This sacred institution included the tabernacle/temple, the priests, and the Levites. To extend the financial support of the Old

Testament temple and its priests to the modern-day church and its ministers is a misapplication. When Jesus fulfilled the law, he replaced both, turning us—you and me—into priests and making us into his temple.

Instead of the old way of doing things, Jesus talked about helping those in need and being wise stewards (Matthew 25:14–29). The early church in Acts shared all they had with each other (Acts 4:32). That's 100 percent. And being a faithful steward of all God has blessed us with also implies 100 percent—all things (1 Corinthians 10:31). We are to use every penny in the best way possible (Matthew 25:14–30).

Whenever the New Testament mentions tithing, it always refers to the Old Testament practice. Nowhere do New Testament writers tell us to give 10 percent to God. And they never command us to donate 10 percent to the local church. Yet this is precisely what many ministers preach.

Instead, we see New Testament commands and examples to use the money God blesses us with to do three things. First is to cover our needs—not our wants (Hebrews 13:5). Next is to help others (1 Corinthians 10:24). And third is to advance God's kingdom (1 Peter 4:10).

Rather than tithing to a church, we see a principle where everything we have belongs to God. We are to be generous stewards of his blessings, in turn using them to bless others (Genesis 12:2). We must use our resources to help those in need and advance God's kingdom, not to support and perpetuate a religious institution.

If you feel a responsible use of God's money is to support your local church, then do so. However, if you think the money is better used somewhere else, then donate to that cause. But never let preachers mislead you—or guilt you—by insisting that you do something the Bible doesn't say to do.

The Status Quo

Yes, it's easy to do what we've always done. It's comfortable to cling to the status quo, but Jesus offers us so much more—and he yearns for us to take hold of it. There is a new way to worship God, to worship him in the Spirit and in truth (John 4:23–24). And this new way doesn't involve attending church each Sunday.

We must stop following the Old Testament model of church: going to a building to meet God, revering the clergy, and tithing out of guilt or obligation. Instead, we should be God's temple, act like priests, and share generously. This is the new model that Jesus gives us.

So why do we persist in going to church to seek God, having a minister serve us, and tithing when Jesus died to give us something new, something much better?

Jesus fulfilled the Old Testament. He offered himself as the ultimate sin sacrifice and then overcame death by rising from the grave. In doing so, he turned us into his temple, promoted us to priests, and changed the 10 percent temple tax into a principle of generosity.

Through Jesus we are his temple and there's no need for a building. We now serve as his priests and there's no need for paid clergy. And last, without a building and staff to finance, there's no longer a need for us to tithe. Instead, we are to help others. This replaces the Old Testament model of church.

Questions: What does it mean for Christians to be Jesus's temple? To serve as priests? How should this inform our church practices?

Chapter 4:

The New Testament Approach to Church

T he commands in the Old Testament about the tabernacle/temple, priesthood, and tithe are clear. The New Testament, however, lacks specific instructions for us to follow. But this doesn't mean we should adhere to the Old Testament model as a default. Instead, we can look at the practices of the early church to guide us in our interactions with God as we worship, serve, and tell the world about Jesus.

Let's start with Stephen, the church's first martyr. In his lengthy message before the Sanhedrin, he reminds those gathered that God does not live in the temple, in a house built by people (Acts 7:48–50). But Stephen isn't spouting a new idea. He quotes Isaiah (Isaiah 66:1–2). This verse finds support from other Old Testament passages (1 Kings 8:27 and 2 Chronicles 2:6).

Even in the Old Testament, God is already correcting his people's idea that he lives in the temple (see 2 Samuel 7:6–7) and that they must go there to engage with him. Remember that God didn't issue his commands about the temple, priests, and tithes until after the people refused to let him speak to them directly and insisted that Moses stand in for them (Exodus 19:6). Could it be that God gave his people the temple, priests, and tithes as a concession to their desire to keep him at a distance?

Interesting.

Regardless, Jesus fulfills this Old Testament way to approach God.

What does this mean for us? What should change? Let's look at the New Testament narrative to gather insight for how to adapt God's Old Testament model of temple, priests, and tithes into a New Testament approach to church.

They Meet in Homes

The first place Jesus's followers meet after he returns to heaven is in the upper room, a part of someone's home (Acts 1:13). They also spend time at the temple (Acts 2:46, Acts 3:1, and Acts 5:20). They visit synagogues on the Sabbath (Acts 9:20, Acts 13:14, and Acts 14:1) and stay until they're no longer welcome

(Acts 18:4–7). They also meet in public spaces (Acts 16:13 and Acts 19:9).

Mostly they meet in people's homes (Acts 2:46, Romans 16:5, 1 Corinthians 16:19, Colossians 4:15, and Philemon 1:2). But this isn't a once-a-week occurrence. They meet daily to share food (Acts 6:1). And they encourage one another (Hebrews 3:13).

The early church continues in their practice of meeting in people's homes for about three centuries. At the end of that time, Constantine legalizes Christianity and begins building churches. This starts a shift from gathering in people's homes—as the early church practiced—to going to dedicated worship spaces—as in the Old Testament.

The book of Hebrews, however, confirms God's intent. It states that the Old Testament tabernacle is an earthly, man-made sanctuary and part of the first covenant (Hebrews 9:1–2). Whereas Jesus, as our high priest, gives us a more perfect tabernacle, one not man-made (Hebrews 9:11).

They Serve as Priests

We've already covered that as Jesus's followers we are his holy and royal priesthood (1 Peter 2:9). John also confirms that Jesus made us to be his priests (Revelation 1:6, 5:10, and 20:6).

In Hebrews we read that just as the priesthood changed—through Jesus—the law must change as well (Hebrews 7:12). In one grand stroke, God's law of the Old Testament becomes Jesus's love in the New Testament. (Not only does the priesthood change in this transition, but so do the accompanying practices of temple and tithe.)

The book of Hebrews reminds us that Jesus is our high priest (Hebrews 3:1). This makes him the ultimate priest, with us looking to him as an example of how to be priests serving under him.

As followers of Jesus we are his priests, a holy priesthood, a nation of priests. Are we doing this? No. Instead, we hire clergy to work as our modern-day priests, serving as our intermediary between God and us. We're not functioning as we should as God's priests. We delegate this holy responsibility to a select few who have put in their time at seminary and received their ordination papers.

Yet God expects us to obey his call to serve as his holy nation of priests. What are we waiting for? What must we do? There are three elements to address in serving our Lord as priests: minister to those in his church, tell others about him, and worship him.

1. Minister to Those in the Church: God intends for all those in his family to serve as priests. We're all priests. This means no one is exempt. Within our church—where everyone is a priest—there's no longer a need for someone to represent God to his people. As priests we can all approach him directly, without the need for an intermediary.

Within the church body, as priests we minister to each other. As Jesus's priests we need to love one another and treat each other as the New Testament tells us to do.

2. Tell Others about Jesus: In the Old Testament, the priests have an inward focus on God's chosen people. They do little to reach out to those outside of their group.

This is one of the things Jesus changes when he fulfills the Old Testament. No longer are we to have an inward focus as his followers, as his priests. Instead, he wants us to look outward.

The resurrected Jesus makes this clear before he returns to heaven. He tells his followers to go throughout the world and make disciples. This includes baptizing them and teaching them about him (Matthew 28:19–20).

Paul—whom God sends to tell the Gentiles about Jesus—acknowledges this is his priestly duty (Romans 15:15–16). As Jesus's priest, Paul tells the Gentiles—that is, non-Jews, which means the rest of the world—the good news of salvation. This is so they can become right with God.

Peter also touches on this in his writing about us being Jesus's priests. He says we are to declare our adoration of Jesus to those living in darkness so we can bring them into his light (1 Peter 2:9).

Jesus instructs us to tell others about him. Paul and Peter say that we do so as his priests.

3. Worship Him: Much of what God establishes in the Old Testament about the tabernacle/temple, priests, and tithes relate to worshiping him. Does this Old Testament worship have a place in the New Testament church?

Yes.

But whereas worship *was* the goal in the Old Testament, it might more so be the means to *reach* the goal in the New. It is when Jesus's church is "worshiping the Lord and fasting" that the Holy Spirit tells them what to do (Acts 13:2). Note that they are doing two things when God speaks to them. It isn't just worship. They also fast. Don't lose sight of this.

Let's consider some other mentions of worship in the New Testament.

We'll start with Jesus and his conversation with the Samaritan woman at the well. She asks about the appropriate place to worship God. Jesus dismisses the discussion about location and says that his followers will worship Father God in the Spirit and in truth (John 4:20–24). This means we can worship God anywhere and don't need to go to a dedicated space. What matters is our attitude toward worship, to do so honestly under the direction of the Holy Spirit.

Just as Peter talks about us offering spiritual sacrifices as our worship (1 Peter 2:5), Paul uses the phrase "living sacrifice." It's holy and pleasing to our Lord, serving as honest and right worship (Romans 12:1).

Paul also testifies that as a part of his faith journey he continues to worship God (Acts 24:11 and 14). Furthermore, in his letter to the church in Corinth, Paul goes into much detail about having orderly worship (1 Corinthians 14). We'll talk more about this in chapter 6.

The author of Hebrews writes about us being thankful for the eternal salvation we received by worshiping God in reverence and awe (Hebrews 12:28–29).

And remember that John's Revelation overflows with worship. This suggests that not only is worshiping God a New Testament act, but it will also be an end times and everlasting practice (Revelation 4:10, 5:14, 7:11, 11:16, 14:7, 15:4, 19:4, 19:10, and 22:8–9).

Yes, we will continue to worship God. But it should look much different than the Old Testament way.

They Give Generously

Not only do Jesus's followers meet in homes and minister to one another, they also have a fresh perspective on giving. Instead of tithing, which isn't a New Testament command, they practice generosity.

The New Testament doesn't mention Jesus's followers taking collections to support the church infrastructure. Instead, they receive offerings to help other disciples in need (Acts 24:17, Romans 15:26, 1 Corinthians 16:1–2, and 2 Corinthians 8). Notice that the focus of their generosity is to those within the church.

The only time the New Testament mentions a weekly collection (1 Corinthians 16:2), it is simply to set aside money to help the struggling believers in Jerusalem, not to support a minister.

They also share what they have with one another (Acts 2:44–45 and Acts 4:32). This is significant, but it isn't a command. Instead, it's an example.

In his letter to the church in Galatia, Paul confirms the importance of helping the poor. In this case, however, he seems to mean all who are poor, both those within the church and those outside (Galatians 2:10).

Jesus talks a lot about money and generosity. He says there will always be poor people among us (Matthew 26:11, Mark 14:7, and John 12:8), but this isn't a reason to not help them. On several occasions Jesus tells people to give money to the poor. He says this to the rich man seeking eternal life (Matthew 19:21, Mark 10:21, and Luke 18:22) and to the Pharisees (Luke 11:41). Finally, Jesus teaches his disciples to help those in need, which we can rightly apply to ourselves as his present-day disciples (Luke 12:33).

There is evidence in the New Testament that the church provides financial support to missionary efforts, though Paul holds up himself as an example of paying for his own expenses as the ideal. He does this even though he feels he has a right to receive financial support as God's messenger (1 Corinthians 9:4–18). Regardless, this financial support is for those who travel to tell the good news of Jesus to those who don't know him, not for local ministers at various city churches.

The New Testament church's practice of generosity is to help the poor and support missionary efforts, not to pay the salaries of local ministers or build and maintain church buildings.

This is the New Testament model for church, Jesus's church. As such, we have much to do.

Jesus frees us from the Old Testament rules about worship. This can move our thinking into an enlightened understanding of church. We see this in the New Testament where Jesus's followers met in homes, ministered to one another, and gave money to help those in need.

Questions: What's one practice of the early church you can personally implement now? Who might you invite to join you in this novel approach? What can you do to better match the generosity modeled by the early church in the Bible?

Chapter 5:

Ten More New Testament Practices

We've already talked about the three main ways Jesus changed our perspectives of following him when he fulfilled the Old Testament prophecies (Luke 24:44). The early church applied this by meeting in homes, serving as priests, and helping those in need. As Jesus's priests, they minister to those in the church, tell others about Jesus, and worship him.

This is a great foundation for how our church today should function. Now let's build on that with ten more characteristics. We can apply these to both our corporate faith gatherings—that is, church—and our personal spiritual practices.

1. Holy Spirit Power and Direction

The Old Testament focuses on God the Father and looks forward to the coming Messiah, Jesus. In the

New Testament, Jesus shows up as the central figure in the Gospels (Matthew, Mark, Luke, and John). Then the Holy Spirit takes over for the rest of the Bible, amplifying what Jesus set in motion. Even so, Jesus is the central figure of Scripture—with God the Father pointing to him and God the Holy Spirit building on what he accomplished. Aside from being the key figure in the Bible, many say Jesus is the most important person in all of history. I agree.

Therefore, to help us establish our ideas of how today's church should function, let's start with Jesus. Doesn't everything begin with him? Jesus does all his work on earth in about three years. He spends that time teaching his disciples and preparing them to take over when he returns to heaven. Despite this, however, they aren't fully ready to assume their critical role when he is ready to leave Earth. Instead, Jesus tells them to wait for the gift of the Holy Spirit.

Jesus says he will ask the Father—his Papa—to send them an advocate to take his place. This advocate will help them now and be with them forever (John 14:16). The Holy Spirit, the advocate, will teach Jesus's disciples everything they need to know, reminding them of the words Jesus spoke when he was here on earth (John 14:26).

In the book of Acts, Luke provides us with added information about this event. Jesus tells his disciples to wait for a gift from Papa. In a few days they will receive Holy Spirit baptism. And his Holy Spirit power will enable them to tell others about Jesus in Jerusalem, the surrounding area, and throughout the entire earth. After saying this, Jesus ascends to heaven, returning to his Father (Acts 1:4–9).

In our church calendar, we call this Ascension Day, the fortieth day after Easter. Ten days later, on Pentecost, we see Jesus's promise of Holy Spirit power fulfilled in dramatic fashion.

The word *Pentecost* only pops up three times in the Bible (Acts 2:1, Acts 20:16, and 1 Corinthians 16:8). This New Testament word doesn't appear at all in the Old Testament. Where did it come from? Pentecost is a Greek word. It means fifty days. Pentecost first occurred fifty days after Jesus's death on Good Friday—and after Jesus instituted the first communion, which occurred on Passover.

Hold that thought.

Let's go back to the Old Testament and look at the Festival of Weeks (Leviticus 23:15–22). It occurs fifty days after Passover. Interestingly, *Festival of Weeks* is an Old Testament phrase and doesn't show up in the New Testament.

The Festival of Weeks in the Bible, also called the Feast of Weeks or the Feast of Fifty Days, is known today as Shavuot. It remembers the day when Moses descends from the mountain with the Ten Commandments and God's laws.

Think about it.

In the Old Testament, fifty days after the first Passover, God gives his people the Law—the rules he expects them to follow.

In the New Testament, fifty days after the first communion—which occurred on Passover—God gives his people the Holy Spirit, his indwelling presence to guide them in following him.

In the Old Testament, God gives his people the Law through Moses. In the New Testament, God gives his people the Holy Spirit through Jesus (Acts 2:1–13).

When the Holy Spirit shows up on Pentecost, everything gets crazy. There's the sound of a rushing wind, the appearance of fire resting on each person, and the disciples speak about Jesus in other languages (Acts 2:1–13).

Some of the people—skeptics—blame it on too much wine.

But the disciples aren't drunk. Peter sets things straight by quoting the prophet Joel: "I will pour out my Spirit on all people" (Acts 2:16–18). The Bible says *all* people. Everyone. Don't miss this.

Joel says it will happen. Peter and the other disciples experience it. And now, how we connect with God changes forever. The Holy Spirit pours himself into *all* of us. Yes, all. That meant them and it means us too—you and me.

Holy Spirit power is the missing element Jesus's followers need before they move forward and advance the kingdom of God. In this, the Holy Spirit plays a leading role. He's prominent in the book of Acts, guiding the early church and empowering its members. Acts mentions the Holy Spirit often, with close to a hundred references. It's clear that the Holy Spirit works in Jesus's place to lead his church.

In one instance, Jesus's followers debate a theological issue about circumcision for new converts.

After they reach a consensus, they write that "it seemed good to the Holy Spirit and to us" (Acts 15:28). Listing the Holy Spirit first suggests that he took a lead role and the people aligned with his perspective. I wonder how often we do just the opposite, where we decide and then try to manufacture Holy Spirit agreement.

Another time, as the church worships and fasts, the Holy Spirit tells them to send out Barnabas and Saul on a missionary journey (Acts 13:2). The Holy Spirit also speaks to Philip (Acts 8:29), Peter (Acts 10:19), Agabus (Acts 11:28), and Paul (Acts 20:22).

But the Holy Spirit isn't just in the book of Acts. He appears in nearly every book of the New Testament, including Revelation. For Jesus's church, the Holy Spirit is in charge. He leads their meetings and directs all that they do.

Just as Jesus is the basis of his church, the Holy Spirit is the catalyst that makes it grow, both 2,000 years ago and now. Jesus gives us the Holy Spirit to empower his church and the people who are part of it. Holy Spirit power should be key in all we do. Through him we're enabled to advance the kingdom of God.

2. Worship

We've already talked a lot about worship. The appropriate worship of God is a central tenet of our faith. The Old Testament mentions worship in 179 verses. The New Testament continues this theme with seventy-five more. Many come from the Gospels as well as Acts. The book of Revelation, however, mentions worship more than any New Testament book and comes in second overall, just behind Deuteronomy.

This makes it clear that worshiping God is in our past, our present, and our eternal future.

In the most profound verse about worship, Jesus reminds us that God is Spirit. Therefore, those who worship him must worship him in the Spirit and in truth (John 4:24).

But what exactly is this verse telling us to do? There are two elements: Spirit and truth.

First, we have the Spirit, with a capital S. This means the Holy Spirit. To fully worship, we must worship through the Holy Spirit. He will direct our worship and guide us. We must follow his lead and do what he says. Though we often think of our worship as a physical act, there is also a spiritual element to it. And the spiritual aspect is the more important one.

Second, we must worship God in truth. This means our worship must be honest and pure. To worship God in truth suggests integrity.

This means that we don't make a show of our worship to impress others or gain their attention. That makes for disingenuous worship and doesn't honor God. It doesn't matter what others think of our worship, it only matters what God thinks.

The opposite of not making our worship a display for other people is holding back our worship for fear of what others may think or say. We must feel free to worship God as the Holy Spirit leads us.

This is how we worship God in Spirit and truth.

3. Prayer

In addition to worship occurring throughout the Bible, we also have prayer. Half of the books in the Old Testament talk about prayer, and most of the books in the New Testament address this subject.

James writes that the prayers of a righteous person are powerful and effective (James 5:16). Paul tells us to pray in all situations (Ephesians 6:18). He also says that everyone should regularly pray (1 Thessalonians 5:17).

The book of Revelation gives us some insight into our prayers. Three times John connects prayers with incense, which God receives from his people. First, we see golden bowls of incense which represent our prayers (Revelation 5:8). Then we have an angel who offers the incense and our prayers before God's throne (Revelation 8:3). And last, we see the smoke of the incense mingling with our prayers, rising to God (Revelation 8:4). Whether we use incense or not, this passage in Revelation gives us a powerful image of how God receives the prayers of his people.

When it comes to praying, however, many people think of the Lord's Prayer. A better label might be the Disciples' Prayer, because Jesus gives the prayer to his disciples as an example of how to pray. It is their prayer, not his.

The Lord's Prayer—sometimes called the Our Father, after its opening line—occurs twice in the Bible. People are familiar with Matthew's version, with many having memorized it and with some churches reciting it as part of their worship practices (Matthew

6:9–13). The version in Luke is far less familiar. It's shorter and more concise (Luke 11:1–4).

Neither of these prayers are for us to recite as much as they are a model for us to follow. Here's an interpretation of how we can apply Matthew's version to inform our prayers.

- We open the prayer by reverencing God.
- Then we ask that his kingdom will come—implicitly with us helping to advance it—and that we will accomplish God's will here on earth.
- In the one personal, tangible request, we ask for our daily bread. That is, we request that God provide for us each day what we need for life. It may be food or something else that's essential.
- Then we ask God to forgive us, just as we forgive others. And if we withhold our forgiveness, this implicitly allows God to withhold it from us. May neither ever happen.
- We end with a request that God will steer us away from temptation and give us victory over Satan's attacks.

- Some versions of the Bible tack on one more phrase. In this we celebrate his kingdom, his power, and his eternal glory.

But this is just one example of how to pray. The key is that prayer is an essential part of our faith journey, both personally and collectively in church.

4. Fasting

Another concept that occurs throughout the Bible is fasting. To fast is to go without food for a time. This isn't an act of mortification to abase ourselves before God or try to gain his attention. Instead, it's to focus our thoughts on him, seeking to better connect with him and align our thinking with his. When fasting, one recommendation is to take the time normally spent eating and use it to pray and listen to the Holy Spirit.

There are two key teachings in the Bible about fasting.

When Jesus instructs the people in his epic message that we call the Sermon on the Mount, he talks about this practice. He says, "*When* you fast . . .", not "*If* you fast . . ." (Matthew 6:16–17). From Jesus's perspective, fasting is not an optional activity but an expectation.

Second, Jesus fasts (Matthew 4:2). In doing so he serves as an example to us all. Since Jesus fasted, is there any reason why we shouldn't?

Interestingly, Jesus doesn't require that his disciples fast, but this is a short-term reprieve because he is with them. He adds that when he leaves, it will be time to resume fasting (Matthew 9:14–15 and Luke 5:33–35). Since he has returned to heaven and is no longer here on earth, it's again time for us to fast.

Jesus wants us to fast, and so we should. We can fast by ourselves or fast with others.

5. Community

The early church also spends a lot of time with each other. This isn't a once-a-week meeting for an hour or two. It may be an everyday occurrence (Acts 2:46, Acts 6:1, and Hebrews 3:13).

They don't live their faith in isolation. They need each other. They need connection. Just as the godhead of Father, Son, and Holy Spirit function as one, so too do Jesus's followers (John 17:20–21 and 2 Corinthians 13:14). Through mutual support they edify one another (1 Thessalonians 5:11). This is how they grow in faith, with iron sharpening iron (Proverbs

27:17). It's two or more people traveling down the road together, keeping each other on the right path and headed in the right direction. It's picking someone up when they stumble (Ecclesiastes 4:9–12).

Living in community is central to who they are and what they do. Without the encouragement and example of others, they'll certainly falter in their faith. Together they are better. Together they can remain focused on Jesus and all he calls them to become. Community is key in making this happen. Think of this as true biblical fellowship (Acts 2:42 and 1 John 1:3–7).

What do they do when they hang out? They spend time in prayer (Acts 1:14, Ephesians 6:18, Colossians 4:2, and James 5:16). They worship (Acts 13:2). They also sing (Ephesians 5:18–20 and Colossians 3:16). The more established disciples of Jesus teach the newer followers about the basics of faith. Think of this as a new members class (Acts 2:42). And we've already covered how they share their material blessings with each other and listen to the Holy Spirit's prompting.

Their functioning in community leads to another trait. They eat together.

6. Breaking Bread

Food is essential to life. Except for when we fast, we eat every day. Most people eat multiple times each day. Though we could eat in solitude, we enjoy food more when in the company of others. Sharing a meal is also a cornerstone of community. This isn't a monthly potluck or an after-church fellowship hour. It's a time of celebration of life around the table.

The New Testament sometimes uses the concept of breaking bread. The phrases "breaking bread," "break bread," and "broke bread" only appear in the New Testament. Should we understand this idea of breaking bread as a synonym for communion or simply for any time people share a meal?

Yes. It's both.

Everyone needs to eat, so why not do it in community? You can gather in homes or meet at coffeehouses and restaurants. Each meal can represent communion—informal, yet relevant, nonetheless. But sometimes you can be more intentional about it. I've had structured communion experiences with other followers of Jesus in homes, and I've celebrated the Lord's Supper at coffee shops. One time our simple passing of bread in Jesus's name served as a witness to the restaurant staff.

We should remember that sliced bread didn't exist two thousand years ago. Though they could have cut bread with a knife, it's more likely that they used their hands—the most convenient tool available to them—to divide a loaf and distribute it to everyone at the meal.

At the world's first communion service, Jesus takes bread and breaks it into pieces so he can pass it out to his disciples. This takes place during the Passover meal (Matthew 26:26, Mark 14:22, and Luke 22:19). Paul references this concept (1 Corinthians 10:16). And we see it used twice in the book of Acts (Acts 2:42 and Acts 2:46).

Yet the idea of breaking bread also refers to an ordinary meal. After Jesus travels down the road to Emmaus with two of his followers, they sit down to eat. Jesus takes the bread, thanks God for it, breaks it into pieces, and passes it out to them (Luke 24:30). Breaking bread, that is, sharing a meal, also occurs after Eutychus falls to his death and Paul brings him back to life. In celebration they share a meal (Acts 20:7 and Acts 20:11).

Another time occurs when Paul is at sea during a terrible storm. The crew and passengers have given up all hope. Paul encourages all the people on board by telling them that though they will lose the ship and cargo, everyone will live. He takes bread, thanks God for it, breaks it, and gives it to everyone to eat, all 276 people (Acts 27:35). Most of the people who eat this bread aren't followers of Jesus. To them this breaking of bread is simply a meal and not a religious rite.

At the first Lord's Supper, Jesus says the bread represents his body, which would soon be broken as part of his crucifixion. At every meal afterward, Jesus's followers would see this breaking of bread, and it would automatically remind them of Jesus's body, broken for them in the ultimate sacrifice. Without speaking a word, the breaking of bread at each meal reminds Jesus's followers of his sacrifice for them.

In this, they see breaking bread as both sacrament and supper. In this sense, communion is a meal, and a meal is communion. May we embrace this understanding just like the early church.

7. Caring for Their Own

The early church shares what they have with one another, and no one has any needs (Acts 2:44–46 and Acts 4:32–35). Notice the focus is on meeting needs, not fulfilling wants. It's critical to distinguish between the two.

Needs refer to what we require to survive, the basics of life: food, clothes, and shelter. Wants are those items that go beyond basic survival requirements. It's essential we help people with their needs, but supplying the things they want is optional.

God has a heart for widows and orphans. He commands we care for them in the Old Testament (Deuteronomy 14:28–29, Psalm 68:5, and Jeremiah 49:11). These instructions carry forward to Jesus's church (James 1:27). Paul adds clarification about caring for widows in his letter to Timothy, writing that a widow's children and grandchildren should put their faith in action by caring for her. However, addressing the needs of widows who have no family members falls to Jesus's church (1 Timothy 5:3–4).

A third example is Jesus's followers in one location taking up a collection to help believers in another. This isn't a command, nor is it a request by those in need. It's a voluntary action by those who feel led by the Holy Spirit to help other believers who struggle (Acts 24:17, Romans 15:26, 1 Corinthians 16:1–4, and 2 Corinthians 8). Interestingly, these are the only times the New Testament talks about taking a collection or receiving an offering of financial gifts. It's to help those in need, not finance a local church.

8. Valuing One Another

Throughout the New Testament we see instructions for how we should treat one another. Let's call these the "one another" commands. We are to:

- Be devoted to one another (Romans 12:10).
- Live in harmony with one another (Romans 12:16).
- Stop passing judgment on one another (Romans 14:13).
- Accept one another (Romans 15:7).
- Instruct one another (Romans 15:14).
- Greet one another with a holy kiss (Romans 16:16, 1 Corinthians 16:20, 2 Corinthians 13:12, and 1 Peter 5:14).

- Agree with one another so that there may be no divisions, perfectly united in mind and thought (1 Corinthians 1:10).
- Encourage one another (2 Corinthians 13:11, 1 Thessalonians 4:18, 1 Thessalonians 5:11, Hebrews 3:13, and Hebrews 10:25).
- Serve one another in love (Galatians 5:13).
- Bear with one another in love. Be completely humble, gentle, and patient (Ephesians 4:2).
- Be kind and compassionate to one another, forgiving each other, just as Jesus forgives us (Ephesians 4:32).
- Speak to one another with psalms, hymns, and spiritual songs (Ephesians 5:19).
- Submit to one another out of reverence for Jesus (Ephesians 5:21).
- Bear with each other and forgive one another (Colossians 3:13). That is, forgive others as Jesus forgives us.
- Teach and admonish one another with all wisdom (Colossians 3:16).
- Build each other up (1 Thessalonians 5:11).
- Spur one another on toward love and good deeds (Hebrews 10:24).

- Keep on loving one another as brothers and sisters (Hebrews 13:1).
- Not slander one another (James 4:11). This includes gossip.
- Not grumble against one another (James 5:9).
- Be like-minded, be sympathetic, love one another, be compassionate and humble (1 Peter 3:8).
- Offer hospitality to one another without grumbling (1 Peter 4:9).
- Act with humility toward one another (1 Peter 5:5).
- Have fellowship with one another (1 John 1:7).
- Wash one another's feet (John 13:14). It's up to us to discern if this is a literal command or a figurative instruction.
- Love one another (John 13:34–35, Romans 13:8, 1 Thessalonians 4:9, 2 Thessalonians 1:3, 1 Peter 1:22, 1 John 3:11, 1 John 3:23, 1 John 4:7, 1 John 4:11–12, and 2 John 1:5).

The last two of these "one another" commands come from the mouth of Jesus. The rest of them are in the letters written by Paul, John, and Peter, as well as the author of Hebrews.

The charge to love one another is the most common of them, mentioned ten times. Jesus, Paul, Peter, and John all tell us to love one another. Jesus says that loving one another is his new command to us (John 13:34–35). Another time Jesus says that the greatest commandment of the Old Testament Law is to fully love God, and the second most important one is to love others as much as we love ourselves (Matthew 22:35–40).

In a world that has multiple meanings for the word love and a distorted understanding of how it functions, what does real love look like? How do we fully love one another? The Bible explains this too.

Paul says that love:

- is patient
- is kind
- does not envy
- does not boast
- is not proud
- is not dishonorable of others
- is not self-seeking
- is not easily angered

- keeps no record of wrongs
- does not delight in evil
- rejoices with the truth
- always protects
- always trusts
- always hopes
- always perseveres

From God's perspective, love never fails (1 Corinthians 13:4–8).

We can then understand love as an overarching principle, a foundation for all others. Paul confirms that love towers over everything else (1 Corinthians 13:13).

As a church, however, we're doing a poor job of following these "one another" instructions. If each person individually did their part to apply these commands in their every-day interactions, our church would be a much different place. And the world in which we live would be better off.

9. Helping Others

We've talked about how we should care for our own and value one another. These examples direct our attention inward, telling us to care for those in Jesus's church and instructing us on how we should act with each other.

This doesn't imply, however, that we should dismiss those outside of our faith community. We should reach out and seek to help them too. As we meet their needs, we have an opportunity to tell them the good news about Jesus (Acts 5:42 and Acts 13:32). This aligns with what Jesus commands (Matthew 28:19–20).

In addition to helping widows and orphans, we're also to show hospitality to strangers (Hebrews 13:2 and 3 John 1:5). Quite simply, a stranger is someone we don't know. This may involve giving them money, but it could also involve helping them receive justice (2 Corinthians 7:11).

Another consideration is to offer them Jesus's healing power. Though healing people in Jesus's name was common in the early church, for many that ability has slipped from their practices today.

The Bible tells about people bringing their ailing friends and placing them on the street where they expect Peter to travel. They hope Peter's shadow might fall on the sick as he passes by. Though the Bible doesn't confirm that people received healing this way, why would they go to this trouble if Peter's shadow hadn't healed others in the past (Acts 5:15)?

Later in the book of Acts, we read about God doing astonishing miracles through Paul. This supernatural power is so extraordinary that even handkerchiefs and aprons that Paul touches contain God's healing power. They bring these garments to people who need healing. The people who receive them are cured and evil spirits are cast out, even though Paul isn't physically present (Acts 19:11–12). Is God still in the business of healing people like this?

Some Christians today claim that supernatural healing power died with the apostles, but there's little biblical support for this position. Jesus says his followers—*all* who believe in him—will do all that he did, including healing people. In fact, we will do even greater things than Jesus (John 14:12). In the book of Acts, we see that *after* people receive supernatural healing an opportunity arises to tell them about Jesus (Acts 3:1–10, Acts 8:6–8, and Acts 9:32–35).

10. Flexible and Informal Leadership

In the New Testament we don't see much indication of a formal leadership structure. Yes, people do serve in leadership roles, but it's not hierarchical or formally instituted. And the various churches never vote on who should lead them. Nor do they hire a minister. So why do we?

After Jesus returns to heaven, the disciples assume a leadership role. This is natural because they know Jesus better than any of the newer converts and are in the best position to teach them (Acts 2:42).

Decision-making in the early church is not democratic. One time they cast lots to pick a leader (Acts 1:26). Another time the people recommend the first deacons. Then the apostles accept who they suggest and pray for them (Acts 6:5–6).

In Acts we see Paul and Barnabas visiting the various churches to appoint leaders. They make their selections through prayer and fasting (Acts 14:23). Paul tells Titus to do the same thing on the island of Crete (Titus 1:5).

But mostly we see people taking initiative, doing what's needed to advance Jesus's church, as led by the Holy Spirit. For example, consider Apollos acting on his own accord to tell others about Jesus (Acts 18:24–25). No one authorizes Apollos to be a missionary. He doesn't need permission. He just acts.

Then Priscilla and Aquila take it upon themselves to expand Apollos's understanding of Jesus (Acts 18:26). And no one appoints them to do it. They see a need, and they meet it.

The early church has a great deal of lay leadership and functions in an almost egalitarian manner. In this, they rely on the Holy Spirit to guide them (Acts 15:28).

The practices of the early church are not commandments to follow, but examples to guide our priorities today. They are descriptive, not prescriptive. In addition to having a fresh understanding on buildings, priests, and tithing, Jesus's church models ten additional practices:

1. *They rely on Holy Spirit power and direction.*
2. *They worship God.*
3. *They pray.*
4. *They fast.*
5. *They pursue community.*
6. *They break bread and eat together.*
7. *They care for their own.*
8. *They value one another.*
9. *They help others.*

10. They have flexible and informal leadership.

Questions: Which of these ten practices would be easiest to implement in your personal faith practice? In a church setting, which would be the hardest? Why? What religious traditions are you willing to break from so that you can practice a more holistic, biblical faith?

Chapter 6:

Five New Testament Ideas
for Church

While considering a better New Testament approach to church in chapter 4, we talked about the three key perspectives that Jesus changed: meeting in homes, serving as priests, and helping those in need. Then in chapter 5 we looked at ten more New Testament practices: relying on the Holy Spirit, worship, prayer, fasting, community, eating together, caring for our people, valuing one another, helping others, and informal leadership.

Now we'll look at five more tangible ideas of church from the pages of the New Testament.

1. The Acts 2 Church

Just days after Pentecost, the people who follow Jesus are hanging out. This is the first church. What do they do?

Luke records their activities:

- They learn about Jesus. Think of this as a new believer's class. Remember, they're mostly all new to their faith in Jesus. This is teaching.
- They spend time with each other. This is community.
- They share meals. This is communion.
- They pray. This is connecting with God.
- They meet every day at the temple where they can find people outside their group. This is outreach.
- They also meet in homes. This is fellowship.
- They share all their possessions. This is generosity.
- They praise God. This is worship.

As a result, more people join them every day. This is what the early church does and how God blesses them (Acts 2:42–47).

What's significant is what they *don't* do. There's no mention of weekly meetings, sermons, music, or offerings. If we're serious about church in its purest form, the early church in Acts 2 gives us much to contemplate when we consider how our church should function today.

2. The Acts 4 Example

As the book of Acts unfolds with its historical narrative of the early church, Luke notes two more characteristics of that church: unity and sharing everything (Acts 4:32).

First, the church is of one heart and mind, just as Jesus prayed (John 17:21). Their actions are consistent with his prayer that they would be one back then, just as we would be one today. Jesus prayed it, and the early church does it. Unity describes what every one of us should pursue and what every church should be. Jesus yearns for us to be united. Over the centuries, Jesus's followers in his church have done a poor job living in unity, as one.

Second, no one claims their possessions as their own. This isn't a mine-versus-yours mentality. Everything is ours. They have a group perspective and act in the community's best interests. They do it out of love for each other. They share everything they have. Not some, not half, but all.

This example is hard for many in our first-world churches to follow today, though not as much for congregations in developing countries. Regardless, while we might do well to hold our possessions loosely, this isn't a command. Later Peter confirms that sharing resources is optional (Acts 5:4).

From Acts 4 we see an example of unity and generosity. This complete generosity, however, is a practice that happens at this snapshot in time for the early church. We will do well to consider how we can apply it today.

3. Paul's Perspective

Now let's look at a third passage. In it, Paul instructs the church in Corinth of how their meetings should proceed (1 Corinthians 14:26–31). While Paul writes to the Corinthian church, we can certainly apply his directives to our practices today.

Paul opens by saying "each of you." This means everyone should participate. The idea of all those present taking part suggests an egalitarian community gathering, where everyone contributes, and everyone ministers to each other.

This removes the divide between leader and follower, which happens in today's church services. During a typical church service today a few people lead, while most people watch. This means that only some are active during the service, while most sit as passive observers, as if going to a concert or attending a lecture.

Instead, Paul wants everyone involved. He lists five activities that should take place.

Sing a Song: First, when we meet, we should sing a hymn or share a song. This could mean playing a musical instrument so that others can sing along. For those who can't play an instrument or lead others in singing, a modern-day option might be to play a recording of a song. Anyone can do that.

Our singing could also mean launching into a song or chorus a cappella as the Holy Spirit leads. This doesn't imply that all our church singing today should be a cappella, but this is something we might want to contemplate.

Teach a Lesson: Second, the same approach applies for giving a word of instruction. We don't need to preach a half-hour to an hour-long sermon. Saying something concisely in thirty seconds may be more meaningful than droning on for thirty minutes. Again, no preparation required. Everyone who's present can do this.

All we need is a willingness to share something God taught us or that we learned through studying

Scripture. In addition, we can rely on the Holy Spirit to tell us what to share during our meeting. It could build off what someone else has already said, or it may be a new topic.

Share a Revelation: Third, the idea of having a revelation to share will seem normal to some and mystical to others. Think of a revelation as special knowledge that God has given to us. He can do this through what we read or things we see. And it can be through Holy Spirit insight. Regardless of the source of our revelation, Paul wants us to share our insights with those gathered.

Speak in Tongues: The last two items in this list may or may not be comfortable activities. The Bible talks about speaking in tongues, and Paul instructs the people in Corinth how to do it. It's biblical, and we should consider this for our church community.

It may be optional, however, because Paul later says, "*If* anyone speaks in a tongue" (1 Corinthians 14:27). This implies that speaking in tongues is not a requirement, but he does give guidelines for when people do speak in tongues (1 Corinthians 14:27–30). We will do well to follow Paul's words.

Interpret the Tongue: After someone speaks in an unknown language, someone must interpret it. Implicitly, if no one can interpret the message, then the person shouldn't share it (1 Corinthians 14:28). After all, how can words that no one understands build up the church (1 Corinthians 14:8–9)?

The Holy Spirit's Role: These five items require no preparation, just a willingness to notice the direction of God's Spirit. This means listening to the Holy Spirit and responding as he directs. Implicit in this is the fact that we will encounter times of silence as we wait and listen. Silence unnerves some people today. But listening to and obeying the Holy Spirit is central to the gatherings of the early church.

Paul says everything we do at our meetings must be for the purpose of building up the church, to strengthen the faith and community of those present. This means not doing or saying anything to elevate ourselves or draw attention to our abilities. Instead, we should humble ourselves and do things for the common good of Jesus's church. This will best advance the kingdom of God and the good news of Jesus.

4. Don't Forget Meeting Together

Note that Paul's instructions to the Corinthian church say *when* you come together, not *if*. This reminds us that gathering with other followers of Jesus should be a regular—not just occasional—occurrence (1 Corinthians 14:26).

The book of Hebrews confirms this idea of regular interaction when it warns us to not give up meeting together. We do this to encourage others to better love and help each other (Hebrews 10:24–25).

This idea of coming together, of meeting with others, can occur on Sunday morning, or it can happen on any other day of the week. The Bible doesn't tell us when to meet. Gathering on Sunday morning is merely a practice that developed over time.

Though many people interpret this instruction to not give up meeting together as a command to attend church, it isn't. Not really. While meeting together can include going to church on Sunday, it should encompass much more. It's a call for intentional interaction with other followers of Jesus. Jesus says anywhere two or three people gather in his name—that is, they get together and place their focus on him—he will join them (Matthew 18:20).

Here are some ideas of how and where we can meet in Jesus's name.

Meals: Most people enjoy meals with others, and most Christians pray before they eat. Isn't this gathering in Jesus's name? While we may eat some meals alone, we potentially have three times each day to connect with others and include Jesus when we eat. But do we make the most of these opportunities?

Coffee Shop: People often meet at coffee shops to hang out. If we include God in our meetings, either explicitly or implicitly, we assemble in his name. Over the years I've had many weekly meetings, both one-on-one and occasionally with groups, in coffee shops. Sometimes the purpose was to instruct people and answer questions, other times it was to mentor them, and occasionally we would simply hang out and enjoy each other's company. It's a low-commitment, easy-to-do activity.

Homes: Do you invite people into your home or see others in theirs? If we both love Jesus, doesn't this become a get-together which includes him? It should.

Outings: What about going on a picnic, to the game, the gym, or shopping? With intentionality, each of these can be another opportunity to meet with others in his name.

Small Groups: Many churches provide opportunities for attendees to form intentional gatherings with a small number of people. This facilitates connection and draws us to God. But this doesn't need to be the result of a formal small group program in our church. We can make our own small group whenever we wish, meeting in the name of Jesus.

Church: Yes, church is on this list of places where we can gather in the name of Jesus. I list it last because it might be the least important. This is because when we go to church, we usually do it wrong. Consider the rest of the verse to find out why.

It says the purpose of meeting together is to encourage one another. People tend to skip that part. The Bible says so, but how often do we do this at our church meetings?

If we leave church discouraged or fail to encourage others while we're there, then we've missed the point of meeting together. While some people make a big deal out of going to church, they forget that the reason is to provide encouragement. If we're not doing that, then we might as well stay home.

5. What Jesus Says

Let's return our discussion to Jesus.

Recall that after Jesus rises from the dead, he tells his followers to stay in Jerusalem, waiting for a surprise Father God has planned for them: the gift of the Holy Spirit to come upon them and give them supernatural power (Acts 1:4–5).

They wait, and the Holy Spirit shows up (Acts 2:1–4). Amazing things happen, and the number of Jesus's followers explodes (Acts 2:41). But after that, they remain in Jerusalem. They're supposed to spread out and share Jesus's good news around the world. He told them to do that too (Matthew 28:19–20). But they don't. They stay put.

They don't realize that God's instruction to wait in Jerusalem doesn't mean they're supposed to stay there forever. Sometimes what God tells us to do is only for a season. Then there's something else for us to do. But if we don't make that transition, we end up being in the wrong place, doing the wrong thing. Instead of staying in Jerusalem—something they're used to and comfortable with—their mission is to go into the world and make disciples (Matthew 28:19–20).

How well are we doing at going into the world and making disciples today? Are we staying put in our church where we're comfortable, or are we looking outside of our Christian community to do what Jesus said to do?

I suspect you know the answer.

Make Disciples: Today's church falls short of being a witness and making disciples. To do so requires an outward perspective, yet most churches have an inward focus. They care for their own to the peril of others. Many churches ignore outsiders completely, sometimes even shunning them.

Yes, God values community and wants us to meet (Hebrews 10:25). And the Bible is packed with commands and examples of worshiping God.

Most churches do the meeting together part, albeit with varying degrees of success. Many of those churches have a time of worship as they meet, though perhaps not always "in the Spirit" or "in truth" as Jesus said to do (John 4:23–24).

Yet few churches look outside their walls to go into their community—let alone the world—to witness and make disciples. Though Jesus said to wait for the Holy Spirit, he didn't say to wait for people to come to us, to enter our churches so we could witness and disciple them. No, we're supposed to leave our Sunday sanctuary to take this Jesus-mandated work to them. We can't do that in a church building on Sunday morning, safely snug behind closed doors.

If we want to make disciples, we need to go out and find them. This brings us to the second part.

Go into the World: There is a time to come together and a time to worship, but there is also a time to go. And we need to give more attention to the going part.

I know of two churches that sent their congregations out into their community on Sunday mornings, forgoing the church service so they could be a church that serves. One church did it a few times and stopped after they saw minimal results and received much grumbling from members. The other church regularly plans this a few times each year and receives a positive reaction from their community.

These were both examples of service initiatives, not outright evangelism. But the best—and easiest—way to talk to people about Jesus is to first serve them in his name.

Every church should make a positive impact on their community. They do this best by entering it. Yet so few do. They're too focused on meeting together and worshiping instead of going out into the world to make disciples. Though you may be reluctant to go into your community on a Sunday morning instead of attending church, what better time to do so? Remember, that's where you'll find the people you want to reach.

We will do well to reform our church practices to conform to these five biblical concepts:

1. *Follow the early church's example to learn about Jesus, pursue fellowship and community, pray and worship, meet daily in public and in homes, and practice kindness.*

2. *Pursue unity and generosity.*

3. *Be ready to rely on the Holy Spirit to sing, teach, share a revelation, speak in tongues, and interpret a tongue.*

4. *Refresh our idea of what it means to meet together.*

5. *Balance our inward efforts on church meetings and worship with an outward focus on going into the world to make disciples.*

Questions: Not including going to a Sunday church service, what can you do to meet regularly with other followers of Jesus? What would it mean for you to practice Jesus's instructions to go into the world (or your community) to make disciples? What tangible actions can you take to put this directive into practice?

Chapter 7:

Seven Things That Must Change

We've looked at how Jesus fulfills the Old Testament to provide a new way for us and our churches to function, replacing the temple, paid clergy, and tithes. Then we explored ten New Testament practices and five New Testament examples to inform our church behavior.

Yet today's church has characteristics that come from our culture and have no scriptural basis. We need to identify these unbiblical practices and remove them from our perspectives—and our churches.

1. Church Is Not about Membership

Membership in a business promotion or club implies privilege. There are qualification requirements to meet. Often there is a fee. Because not everyone can meet these barriers to entry, membership becomes a status symbol. It separates those who are in from those who are out.

Church does the same thing when it touts membership. To become a church member, there are hoops to jump through: attend classes, agree to certain teachings, follow specific rules, or commit to give money, possibly even at a certain annual level.

Once we become a member, the church accepts us as one of its own. They fully embrace us, and we become one of them. We are elite, and, even if we won't admit it, we swell with pride over our special status. Now the church and her paid staff will care for us. To everyone else, they offer tolerance but withhold full acceptance. That's because church membership has its privileges.

There's one problem.

Church membership is not biblical. We made it up.

Having members separates church attendees between those on the inside and everyone else. It pushes away spiritual seekers. Membership splits the church of Jesus, separating people into two groups, offering privileges to one and holding the other at a distance.

It is a most modern concept, consumerism at its finest. (More on this in the next section.)

Although well intended, membership divides the church that Jesus wants to function as one (John 17:21). Jesus loves everyone, not just those who follow him or give money. Paul never gives instructions about church membership, Peter never commands we join a church, and John never holds a new membership class.

2. Church Is Not for Consumers

When we join a church by becoming a member, we expect something in return. In addition to acceptance, we seek benefits. That's why we go church shopping, striving to find the church that offers us the most. We look for the best preaching, the most exciting worship, and the widest array of programs to meet our needs.

This is consumerism—and it doesn't belong in the church.

When people feel free to leave a church, often over the smallest of slights, they view themselves as a customer shopping for the church that offers the most value. This is a consumer mindset, not a godly perspective.

We shouldn't shop for a church that provides the services we want. Instead, we should look for a faith community we can help.

When people go church shopping, the church becomes a service provider. Which church offers the best services? Then the focus shifts to programs, service styles, and preaching power.

This idea of receiving services influences our church selection process. Seldom do people look for a church that gives them the opportunity to serve. Instead, they seek a church for the benefits it provides: the music, the message, and the ministries. They're church shoppers, pursuing church selection with a consumer mindset.

The result is a retail religion. These people shop for a church the same way they buy a car or look for a gym. They make a list—either literally or figuratively—of the things their new car, gym, or church *must* have. Then they draft their wish list of what they hope their new car, gym, or church *could* have. And then they create a final list of deal breakers, detailing the things their new car, gym, or church *can't* have.

Then they go shopping.

They tick off items on their list. With intention, they test drive cars, check out gyms, or visit churches. In each case, they immediately reject some and consider others as possibilities. Eventually they grow tired of shopping and make their selection from the top contenders, seeking a solution that provides them with the most value.

I've done this. Twice.

Both times my reason for leaving sounded spiritual, but it was a ruse. I was being a self-centered consumer. The first time my justification for going church shopping was, "We're just not being fed here anymore." Never mind that it's not the church's role to feed us spiritually. We're supposed to do that ourselves.

The other time it was, "They're not meeting our family's needs." I sought a church with programs relevant to my family. Yes, getting our children plugged into a good youth group was important, but that didn't require changing churches. Our kids had other options, but we didn't see these alternatives.

A better, and more God-honoring, approach is to seek a church community that provides opportunities for us to serve. We need to stop thinking of church for the things it will provide for us and instead consider the things we can do for it, that is, for the people who go there and the community surrounding it.

We should look for a church that provides opportunities for us to serve, according to how God has wired us, in ways that make us come alive. This includes service within the church and to those people outside the church.

Service is not an isolated activity. As we serve, we do so as a group. Church service and community matter more than church programs and benefits.

Instead of asking, "What can the church do for me?" the better question becomes "What can I do for the church?" Don't seek to be served but to serve. (See Matthew 20:28 and Mark 10:45.)

3. Church Is Not about Division

We've talked about how church membership divides people. Some carry the special status of members, while others are relegated to second-class status as attendees. Membership segregates people into two groups. This divides Jesus's church, the body of Christ.

Sadly, there are nuances within membership too. There are those who serve on boards and committees and those who don't function in a leadership capacity. There are those who teach classes and those who don't. There are those who volunteer and those who don't. Each distinguishing characteristic elevates some and devalues others.

We also divide by race, ethnicity, and socioeconomic status. More God-dishonoring segregation. Shame on us.

Before Jesus sacrifices himself for us, he prays that we will be one, just as he and the Father are one (John 17:20–21). If we are one, we are united. There is no room for division.

4. Church Is Not about Theology or Doctrine

Another way we promote division is through our theology and our doctrine. Yes, theology divides us. Even more so, our doctrine.

At its most basic level, theology is the study of God. Doctrine is the application of that theology.

But the modern idea of finding the right theology, followed by the unassailable doctrine, piles layers on top of these two basic understandings. The subject gets murky. The result is too many multi-syllable words that few people can pronounce and even fewer can comprehend. Turning God into an academic pursuit of the right theological doctrine pushes him away and keeps us from truly knowing him. The ideal purpose of theology is to move us into a relationship with God.

Imagine if I went to my wife and said, "I'm going to devote the rest of my life to studying you. I'll watch you and make notes. I'll catalog who you are and categorize what you do. Next, I'll read books to help me better understand you. I'll also talk with others to gain their insights about who you are. Then I'll tell people what I've learned."

How would she react? Not well.

My singular commitment to focus on her would not win me her appreciation. Instead, she would rightfully complain, "Why can't we hang out? I just want you to spend time with me."

So it is with God. He doesn't want us to study him. He wants a relationship (Hosea 6:6). Yet how the church applies their theology inevitably produces rules. These rules serve to keep God at a distance when what he really wants is for us to know him.

When most people pursue theology, they amass information. Much of this forms a theoretical construct, turning God into an abstract spiritual entity. They gather knowledge at the risk of pushing the Almighty away. This knowledge of who God is generates pride. It puffs up. Instead of knowledge, we should pursue love, which builds up (1 Corinthians 8:1).

The pursuit of theological learning is a noble task, but it's not the goal. Chasing after a theology of God and the right doctrine isn't the end. Theology is the means to the end: to know who God is in an intimate, personal way. In this regard, doctrine doesn't matter.

Instead of helping us move into relationship with God, we take our doctrines and make labels to identify specific religious streams of thought. Then we use these labels to judge others, deeming them as aligned with our thinking or opposed to it. This fractures Jesus's church, which he yearns to see function as one (John 17:20–21). We cite certain beliefs as immutable. We fellowship with those who agree with us and disassociate from those who disagree. We dishonor Jesus in the process, and, as a result, we serve as poor witnesses.

One church I attended refused to promote an outreach event at a like-minded congregation. They made their determination over a doctrinal difference that our church leadership didn't (or couldn't) explain. It makes me wonder if their decision wasn't a personal dispute masked as a spiritual issue. Ironically, the church they rejected had founded them twenty years prior. It would be funny if it weren't so sad.

Jesus desires that we, his followers, *all* get along, that we co-exist in unity. That doesn't mean churches should be conflict free. This is impossible. Even the early church in Acts had disagreements, but they worked through them to resolve their differences and remain united.

When our churches today preach doctrine, they drive a wedge into the body of Christ. As a result, our differing creeds separate us. This harms Jesus's church and damages our witness to the world. A doctrine that divides has no place among Jesus's followers.

Jesus is what matters. Everything else is secondary.

5. Church Is Not for Networking

Some people become part of a church to make marketing contacts or achieve status as a member of a high-profile congregation. Their goal in attending isn't spiritual. It's business. It's closing sales. And once they've sold all they can to those who attend that church, they move on to another one. For them attending church is a business strategy, and God takes a backseat.

Yes, I've been on the receiving end of people using church connections for business networking. The most hurtful of these was a young couple who reached out to me and my bride when we taught their young daughter in Sunday school. We were elated when they invited us to their home. That's when I learned they had just joined a multilevel marketing company. I asked them if that was the reason for the invite. They confirmed it was and said it would be foolish for us not to consider this amazing, life-changing opportunity they were offering. We declined, and they never talked to us again. They soon switched churches.

6. Church Is Not a Business

The triple aim of most churches—attendance, offerings, and facility—doesn't matter as much as most people think. Said more bluntly, most church leaders today focus on the three Bs: butts (in the chairs), bucks (in the offering), and buildings. The congregation buys into this without hesitation. These measures of success become the focus. But this focus is off, even looking in the wrong direction. This is a worldly perspective, a business mindset.

But a church is not a business, and we shouldn't run it like one either. Many churches today, however, think like a business and operate like one. A church should not have a profit motive, that is, maximizing donations. Nor should a church adapt current business world concepts such as having a CEO, a board, marketing strategies, customer experience, and incentive programs.

Yes, a church should be fiscally responsible and manage its money—God's money— with the highest integrity. And a church needs some degree of leadership, but remember Jesus modeled the idea of servant leadership (Matthew 20:28 and Mark 10:45). So should today's church leaders.

We shouldn't track the achievements of our church the same way a corporation would. Today's church measures success by attendance, offerings, and facility size. This is because the world values increased scope: the number of people, amount of money, and square footage.

As an entrepreneur with a lifetime of business experience, I've made the mistake of trying to treat churches with the same mindset that I used to run companies. My perspective was in error, and no one called me out on it. In fact, most applauded my business insight and how I tried to apply it to church.

We're more like the world than we care to admit. We think more people showing up for church each week is good. A larger campus impresses. Bigger offerings allow for more of the same. Churches with a sizable attendance or grand edifice garner attention. They receive media coverage. Books celebrate them and put their leaders on lofty pedestals.

This is how the Western world defines success.

But I doubt God cares about the size of our audience, offerings, or facility. Instead of an unhealthy, unbiblical focus on the three Bs, what if we and our churches looked to the three Cs of changed lives, community, and commitment?

Changed Lives: First, Jesus wants changed lives. He yearns for us to repent (Luke 13:3) and follow him (Luke 9:23). Then we can reorder our priorities. In fact, almost everything he says is about changing the way we live.

Community: Next, Jesus wants to build a community—to be one—just as he and his Papa are one (John 17:21). He yearns for us to be part of the kingdom of God (John 3:3). Instead, we became a church.

Commitment: Lastly, Jesus expects our commitment. He desires people who will go all in. He wants us to follow him, to serve him, and to be with him (John 12:26). We need to maintain our focus on him and not look back to what we left behind (Luke 9:62). That's commitment, and that's what Jesus wants.

If Jesus focuses on changed lives, community, and commitment, so should we. Let's push aside butts, bucks, and buildings, because these things get in the way of what Jesus wants for his followers.

7. Church Is Not an Institution

Most churches—and especially denominations—become institutions over time. I oppose denominations. They are a result of division, and they perpetuate division. Denominations are the antithesis to the unity Jesus prayed for.

Churches, as institutions, seek to perpetuate themselves regardless of the circumstances. In their struggle for survival, they lose sight of why they existed in the first place. Instead of seeking to serve their community and share salvation through Jesus, their focus turns inward. Their priority is on self-preservation at all costs.

People expect a church—their local church—to last forever. They forget that a congregation, comprised of people, is a living, breathing, and changing entity. It's organic. This means that individual churches—unlike the universal church—are born, grow, thrive, and die, just like the people who are in them.

The only way to avoid this is for a church to become an institution, but once it does it loses its original purpose. It's no longer alive. It's dead and can do little to advance the kingdom of God.

Church shouldn't be a business, institution, or club. We must rescind membership, stop thinking like consumers, and pursue unity over segregation. Finally, we need to stop dividing ourselves by our theology and our doctrine. Jesus has one church. We must start acting like it.

Questions: Which of the seven church errors is most reflected in your congregation? What personal perspective do you most need to change? What steps can you take to reorient your own practices and help your local church do the same?

Chapter 8:

Church Keys

Aminister once said in his Sunday morning
message that some people go to church
for the music and put up with the sermon.
Others go for the sermon and put up with the music.
The minister's statement suggests that people feel a
church service has two primary elements. One is the
worship music, and the other is the sermon.

I get this. At one point in my life I endured the
singing as I waited for the sermon. Then my perspective flopped as I pursued worship and endured the
teaching. Now neither matters too much to me.

In recent years I haven't gone to church for the music or the message. I show up for the chance to experience meaningful community before or after the service.

Put Music or Message in Its Place

Though the New Testament talks about both music
and message, neither seems central to their meetings,

especially not the way we pursue these two items today.

Music: Though music is a part of Jesus's church in the Bible, it emerges more as a secondary pursuit. Paul doesn't ascribe music to a worship leader but to each person gathered. The purpose of this is to build up Jesus's church (1 Corinthians 14:26). Music is part of the "one another" commands as a way of ministering to each other (Colossians 3:16 and Ephesians 5:18–19).

An interesting side note is that the New Testament never mentions using musical instruments in their worship of God, as happened throughout the Old Testament. Also, sometimes New Testament singing to God happens apart from a church gathering, such as when Paul and Silas are sitting in jail (Acts 16:25). Let's consider how we can apply their example to our reality today.

Sometimes the music set at one of today's church services is worshipful, drawing us into closer fellowship with God. But too often it's more of a performance for attendees than a tribute to our Creator. This makes the music portion of some church services more akin to a concert, even to the point of including a light show, smoke machines, and accompanying video projection behind the performers.

And if you claim your church worship time isn't a performance, then why are the singers and musicians positioned in front of everyone and elevated on a stage? With today's sound systems, the artists could be located anywhere. If the music is truly a tribute to God and not a performance for us, then why not station the musicians behind the congregation or out of sight so their presence won't distract us from God?

Message: A friend of mine calls the church sermon a lecture. I'm not sure if he's joking or serious, but I get his point. I've heard sermons that so sidestepped the Bible, faith, and the good news of Jesus that the resulting words were no different than a lecture from a secular speaker.

There are, however, three specific instances where New Testament writers describe activity that we might equate to a sermon.

The first is educating people about their faith (Acts 2:42). This implicitly is for new believers, giving them spiritual milk as we would feed a baby (1 Corinthians 3:1–3). This basic training grows them in their salvation (1 Peter 2:1–3). And it prepares them to teach others (Hebrews 5:11–14). It's not something to persist in doing Sunday after Sunday. Instead, it's a temporary situation we should grow out of.

Most people cringe at the implication that mature followers of Jesus don't need a minister to teach them. They worry that heresy will inevitably result. At first this seems valid, but in truth, most major heresies throughout history have come from trained, ordained ministers whose teachings went unchallenged by their followers.

In truly egalitarian faith communities, however, if one participant veers toward an unbiblical (heretical) teaching, their peers are quick to offer correction as guided by the Bible and influenced by the Holy Spirit. This means that movements toward heresy tend to be self-correcting in a community of equals without the need for a professional minister.

The second reason to have a church message is for missionaries to tell those outside the church about Jesus. This can't happen at a church meeting because those who need to hear the good news of Jesus aren't there. Spreading the gospel message requires going out to encounter people where they are, not expecting them to come to us and our church services (Acts

8:4, Acts 8:40, Romans 10:14–15, and 2 Corinthians 10:16).

And the third is traveling missionaries who give updates at the local churches (Acts 14:27, Acts 15:4, and Acts 20:7).

Everyone Participates: Regarding these two elements of music and message—things we place so much emphasis on in our churches today—Paul gives instructions to the church in Corinth. It's not the job of a worship leader to lead us in song. Nor is it the role of a minister to preach a sermon. We—the people in attendance—are to do these things, and more, for each other. It's an egalitarian gathering where we all take part for our common good to build up Jesus's church (1 Corinthians 14:26).

Remember, through Jesus, we are *all* priests. It's time we start acting like it.

Community

What does show up as a recurring theme throughout the New Testament is community. We talked about this in chapter 5 and gave examples in chapter 6. Now we'll expand on it.

Community goes way beyond the time of personal interaction that I seek before or after a Sunday service. The church, as a group of people, should major on community, on getting along and experiencing life together. Community should happen before, during, and after each of our gatherings—those on Sunday, as well as those throughout the week. In all that we do, community must be our focus. We should enjoy spending time with each other, just hanging out.

If we don't like spending time with the people we see for an hour each Sunday morning, then something's wrong—not with them, but with us. Yes, community can get messy. But we have Jesus's example, the Holy Spirit's insight, and the Bible's wisdom to guide us in navigating the challenges that erupt when people spend time with each other in intentional interaction.

Here are some of the aspects of community that we see in the early church, and that we can follow in today's church.

Share Meals: A lot of eating takes place in Jesus's church. We must feed our bodies to sustain us physically, so why not do it in the company of other like-minded people? In community, sharing food becomes a celebration of life and of faith. (See "Breaking Bread" in chapter 5.)

Fast: Although Jesus's followers do a lot of eating together, they also fast (Matthew 6:16–17 and Acts 14:23). Fasting is an intentional act of devotion that helps connect us with God and align our perspectives with his. Remember that although Jesus's disciples didn't fast, once he left, it was time for his followers to resume fasting (Luke 5:33–35).

Prayer: Another reoccurring New Testament theme is prayer. This isn't a minister-led oration on Sunday morning. This is more akin to a mid-week prayer meeting, with everyone gathered in community to seek God in prayer together (Acts 1:14 and Acts 12:5).

Listen to the Holy Spirit: As the people pray, sometimes associated with fasting, they listen to the Holy Spirit (Acts 15:28). Then they obey what the Holy Spirit calls them to do (Acts 13:2–3).

Minister to One Another: In their community they follow the Bible's "one another" commands, which teach us how to get along in a God-honoring way. (See "Value One Another" in chapter 5.)

Serve Others: We serve one another in our faith community (Galatians 5:13). We should also serve those outside our church, just as Jesus served others. And we shouldn't serve with any motive other than with the pure intent to show them the love of Jesus. Loving others through our actions may be the most powerful witness we can offer. We need to let our light shine so that the world can see (Matthew 5:14–16 and James 2:14–17). All of humanity is watching. May they see Jesus in what we do (1 Peter 2:12).

Tell Others about Jesus: The New Testament gives examples of people telling others about Jesus in their local community (Acts 3:11–26 and Acts 7:1–53). It also mentions sending people out into the world as missionaries (Acts 8:4–5 and Acts 13:2). Witnessing, both local and abroad, springs from the foundation of community.

Unity

In our community we should pursue harmony. Jesus prayed that we would be one (John 17:20–21). The early church modeled unity (Acts 4:32). We also covered their consensus in "The Acts 4 Example" in chapter 6.

When issues arise among Jesus's followers that threaten their singlemindedness, they work through it to avoid division (Acts 11:1–18). This unity includes working out any disagreements over doctrine (Acts 15:1–21).

We need to rethink what happens at our church, deemphasizing the significance of music and message while elevating the importance of community, one that functions in unity for Jesus.

Questions: How can you change your view of church music and message? What steps can you take to pursue meaningful Christian community? How can you better promote Christian unity to *all* of Jesus's followers?

Chapter 9:

Perspectives We Must Change

So far, we've looked at the Old Testament model for church—of buildings, paid clergy, and tithes—which we still follow today. Then we considered how Jesus fulfills the Old Testament and looked at how the early church functions in the New Testament, considering their practices and detailing what church shouldn't be today. In the last chapter, we looked at the essential components for a New Testament-style church.

Now we'll look at some supporting elements. We'll consider what must change in our churches today to better align with the New Testament narrative and early church practices. We've already touched on this in chapter 3 when we said that through Jesus, we have a new perspective on the temple (church building), priests (ministers and staff), and tithes and offerings (church finances).

Building

Who needs a building? The early church met in people's homes and public places. Why can't we do the same today? Think of all the money we'd save and the hassles we could avoid if we removed the shackles of owning and maintaining a church facility.

Not only are our church structures exorbitantly expensive, but they're also underutilized most of the time. At best, one of today's churches enjoys full usage for only two hours of each week. That's 1.2 percent of the time. This means that for 98.8 percent of each week the building is hardly used.

Yes, the office staff uses a tiny part of the space during the workweek, and smaller meetings occur some evenings. But these activities occupy only a small portion of the building. That's a lot of wasted space. The prime motivation for these large, but underused, facilities is for a one-hour church meeting each Sunday.

At one church I visited, the pastor in his pre-sermon prayer pleaded with God to supply a facility for them. "You know, God, how much we *need* a building," he begged. "Please provide it for us." Although their rented space offered what they needed on

Sunday morning and other options provided office space and accommodated their weekly meetings, it appeared that his perspective was that to be a real church they had to have a building. For him, owning a church building to meet in was an imperative part of his congregation's future.

In a later discussion with one of their church elders I said, "You don't need a building. You may *want* one, but you don't *have* to have one." She considered my words and then agreed, wondering aloud how she might share this insight with her pastor.

In most cases, it costs a church much less to rent space than to own and maintain a building. But even better than renting space for Sunday morning services is to decentralize the church to meet in people's homes.

Despite this, most every church thinks they need a building. While owning a building is convenient and may be a preference, it isn't a necessity. And sinking mass quantities of money into a building that goes unused most of the week certainly isn't being a good steward of God's resources.

In today's developed countries churches routinely spend millions of dollars for a worship space for people to go to on Sunday morning. The cost of the facility is disproportionately large in comparison to the lifestyles and homes of the congregation.

In another instance, a large, growing suburban church had frequent building fund drives to expand its facility. Though the people enthusiastically supported each expansion plan, one effort met with opposition. They wanted to raise $1 million to build a ring road around the campus to ease the flow of traffic. One million dollars for a road. It was a hard ask for the people to accept.

Even in developing countries, where the expectations of the church edifice are much more modest, it's still disproportionate to the lifestyle of the people who will go there. In one developing country, a church constructed the concrete shell for its building and ran out of money. For several years, they've worshiped in their half-finished space and continually asked for donations to complete its construction. Since the members are poor, they can't finance the construction themselves. Instead, they look to the generosity of those outside their community to complete the building. Instead of focusing his attention on his congregation and local community, the pastor diverts some of his time to solicit donations from those abroad.

Regardless of where we live in the world, our church structures are expensive compared to the lifestyles of most of the people who go there. To have our facility, we must either buy or build. This often requires borrowing money and paying off a mortgage. And if a church falls behind on their monthly payments, the lender may have no choice but to foreclose on the facility. In this instance, no one wins, and the reputation of Jesus's church is tarnished.

But expenses don't stop with the acquisition of a building, whether bought or built. The ongoing costs add up. For starters, there are utilities, maintenance, and insurance. And we do all this so we can go to a place to have a one-hour encounter with God on Sunday morning.

Maintaining a church building is costly and does little to advance the kingdom of God. Remember, through Jesus, our bodies are God's temple, a dwelling place of the Holy Spirit (1 Corinthians 6:19–20). We don't need to go to a building to go to church so we can connect with God. We take church with us wherever we go—or at least we should.

Staff

In chapter 7 we mentioned that the church should not be an institution. Yet most churches today move in that direction after about ten years of operation, and they become an institution a couple of decades after that. For an institution to work, it needs paid staff (and money). That's why local pastors receive a salary: to keep the institution of church functioning and viable.

As we've already covered, this thinking follows the Old Testament model of church. But we don't live in the Old Testament or under its covenant. We live in the New Testament and under *its* covenant—at least in theory. In the New Testament, those who follow Jesus are his church. Each one of us is a priest—that is, a minister—to care for one another. We shouldn't pay someone to do what we're supposed to do. As part of the body of Christ, we each do our part to advance the kingdom of God and shouldn't expect to receive payment for our labor.

Missionaries: There is, however, one exception to this idea of no compensation. In his letter to the people in Corinth, Paul builds a case to pay missionaries. This doesn't apply to the folks who run local churches but to those who go around telling others about Jesus. Today, we might call these people evangelists. Based on Paul's teaching, it's right to pay them.

Yet once Paul builds his case to appropriately pay missionaries, he points to an even better way: for missionaries to earn their own money and not require outside support. Paul often covers his expenses and those traveling with him by plying his trade. He works as a tentmaker. Springing from this is the idea of a tentmaker-missionary, someone who pays their own way as they tell others about Jesus (1 Corinthians 9:7–18).

Local Ministers: But what about the local church? Shouldn't we reward our clergy by paying them? Doesn't the Bible say that workers deserve compensation (1 Timothy 5:18)? Not quite. The context of this is for traveling missionaries to be content with the food and lodging provided to them as they journey about telling others about Jesus (Luke 10:5–7).

But don't we need a minister to teach us about God each Sunday? No. The Bible expects us to feed ourselves spiritually. And we are to teach one another.

What about a clergy member to address our spiritual needs as they arise? No. We are to care for one another.

No Payroll: In short, through Jesus the institution of church is over—at least in principle. Without a physical building or an institution to maintain, there is no need to pay someone to run the whole show.

So if you are part of an institution and want to perpetuate it, then buy a building, hire staff, and pay them their due. However, if you want to pursue a different path, as seen in the New Testament, then take the church with you wherever you go and help others however you can, paying your own way as you do.

Money

The Old Testament church required a lot of support to keep it going. There was a tabernacle to build and transport. The temple later replaced the tabernacle, but it required regular maintenance. The priests and Levites received support too.

This huge need required the people to give their tithes and various offerings, some mandatory and others voluntary. In today's church, facility costs and payroll expenses make up most of the church's budget, sometimes all of it. Yet if we were to do away with these two elements, there's not so much need for money.

After building and staffing costs, what small amount remains in the budget falls into two categories. First is benevolence, that is, taking care of our own just like the early church did. Second is outreach, sending missionaries out to tell others the good news about Jesus (Matthew 28:19–20, Mark 16:15–16, and Luke 14:23). Think of all the good a church could do with its money if it directed 100 percent of its funds to these two activities and didn't need to pay for a facility and staff.

In the New Testament church, people share what they have to help those within their spiritual community, that is, those within their church. They seldom take offerings, and when they do it's to help other Jesus followers who suffer in poverty. The third thing they do with their money is fund missionary efforts. Instead of constructing buildings and paying staff, they help people and tell others about Jesus. It's that simple.

Rather than focusing on 10 percent, as the Old Testament prescribes, we should reframe our thinking to embrace the reality that all we have, 100 percent, belongs to God. We are to be his stewards to use the full amount wisely for his honor, his glory, and his kingdom—not *our* honor, glory, and kingdom.

Paul writes that the love of money is a source of all manner of evil. An unhealthy preoccupation with wealth is especially risky for followers of Jesus, as our pursuit of accumulating wealth can distract us from our faith and pile on all kinds of grief (1 Timothy 6:10).

Keep in mind that Paul is not condemning money. He warns against the *love* of money. For anyone who has accumulated financial resources, this serves as a solemn warning to make sure we have a God-honoring understanding of wealth and what its purpose is. When it comes to the pursuit of possessions—our love of money—we risk having it pull us away from God.

We need money to live, but we shouldn't live for the pursuit of wealth. We should use money to supply our needs, help others, and serve God. Consider these three areas:

First, we need God's provisions to take care of ourselves (2 Thessalonians 3:10). We must focus on what we *need*, not what we *want*.

Second, we should use our financial resources to help fund the things that matter to God. This means we need to understand his perspective.

With the wise use of our money, we can serve God and honor him. We must remember that we can't serve two masters: God and money (Matthew 6:24).

Third, we should consider others. What do they need? How can we help them? Again, as with our own balancing of needs versus wants, we must guard against supplying someone with what they want, instead of focusing on what they truly need. God especially desires that we help widows and orphans (James 1:27). He also has a heart for us to help foreigners and the poor (Zechariah 7:10).

Therefore, we should give to God first (Exodus 23:19). Then we should concern ourselves with our needs and helping others with theirs. God wants our best, not what's left over. This applies to our possessions and our actions.

Does this mean we need to give to the local church? Maybe. But it's much more than that. We must direct our money, as wise stewards, to where it can have the most kingdom impact. I question if this means supporting an organization where most—or all—of its budget goes to paying for buildings and staff.

Membership

Once we reform our perspectives on church buildings, staff, and donations we can then address some secondary issues. The first is church membership. As we covered in chapter 7, it's not biblical. Membership is something that almost everyone in church accepts without question. But we should question it.

Church membership has no scriptural basis. Nowhere does Jesus tell us to go out and find members, make members, or sign up new members. Increasing membership is simply not a biblical mandate. In fact, the word membership doesn't even occur in the Bible. It's something well-meaning religious leaders made up. It may seem like a wise idea, but it's not.

Membership establishes two levels within Jesus's church. We must repent of making this distinction. Membership causes division among Jesus's followers, segregating attendees into two classes of people, the insiders who are members from those on the periphery, the nonmembers.

Some churches, attempting to correct the fallacy of church membership, have come up with new labels. I've heard them use the terms *missionaries*, *partners*, and *associates*. I'm sure there are more.

These perspectives, though well intended, are merely different names for the same membership problem. The result is that church membership still creates two classes of people in Jesus's church: insiders and outsiders.

At some churches, baptism makes this membership distinction. Once a person undergoes the rite, or sacrament, of baptism—often by immersion— they automatically become a member. If they are underage at the time, they might not become a voting member until they reach adulthood. This produces a third class of attendees, a third division in Jesus's church: non-voting members.

Jesus welcomes all (Romans 15:7, Galatians 3:28, and James 2:1–4). We should do the same, ditching church membership as an ill-conceived, man-made tradition that has no scriptural basis.

We must resist the human tendency toward membership, which segregates people, and instead embrace God's perspective of inclusion. Instead of encouraging church membership, we should promote Christian unity.

Seminary

Most churches expect their paid clergy to have undergone formal, academic education. Many insist on a seminary degree. From a worldly standpoint this makes sense. But from God's perspective I can imagine him laughing. Look at the credentials of Jesus's twelve disciples. They were ordinary people, having received no higher education beyond that of most Hebrew children. Their one essential qualification is that they spent time with Jesus.

I repeat: Their one essential qualification is that they spent time with Jesus.

Though today's leaders can't spend physical time with Jesus, they can in the spiritual sense. Walking with Jesus in an intimate way and having his Holy Spirit lead them—just like in the Bible—is what we most need from our church leaders today.

Instead, today's seminaries focus on an academic deep dive into the Bible, ensuring that graduates overflow with a substantial theological foundation, something most church members care little about. Seminary best prepares graduates to teach other seminary students. It falls short in equipping its students to provide the type of ministry functions that people at churches want. Even worse, I fear formal religious education downplays having a relationship with Jesus and following the Holy Spirit, making these traits secondary in importance.

We need to select our clergy based on their godly character and not their seminary diploma.

Sunday School

It may seem strange to see Sunday school on this list of things we must change, but we should carefully reexamine it. The Bible tells parents—not the church—to instruct their children (Deuteronomy 4:9–10, Deuteronomy 11:19, Proverbs 22:6, and Ephesians 6:4). Yet Sunday school operates despite these biblical commands.

Do you know the original mission of Sunday school? It was to teach poor children how to read. And the church used the most accessible reading text, the Bible. By the time public schools came into existence and took over this job of teaching children how to read, Sunday school had become entrenched in churches. Instead of realizing they had accomplished their objective and shutting it down, Sunday school shifted its focus to teach the church's children about God. It didn't matter that this was the parent's responsibility (Ephesians 6:4).

We could use this as scriptural justification for shutting down our Sunday schools, but a better approach might be to reform Sunday school into a program to help those in our community, as originally intended. One example that would apply in many areas of the United States is to look at teaching English as a second language (ESL). Though many ESL programs already exist, they don't reach everyone. But regardless of the focus, the church should reform their Sunday school practice to address needs in their community.

Division, Disunity, and Denominations

Just as church member status divides the church body into two groups, so does our doctrine. We make a lengthy list of what we should do and shouldn't do, judging others according to our opinions of what's proper and what's not. This legalistic approach follows what the Old Testament set in motion with its 613 instructions of things to do and not do in the Law of Moses. Compounding the problem, God's children in the Old Testament added tens of thousands of man-made rules, which evolved over the centuries, to help interpret the original 613 expectations God gave to Moses.

Jesus says that his yoke is easy, and his burden is light (Matthew 11:30). This means his doctrine is simple to follow and effortless to bear. To confirm this, Jesus simplifies all these Old Testament commands and man-made traditions when he says we are to love God and love others (Luke 10:27). Yes, Jesus's essential expectation is love.

To accomplish these two instructions to love God and love others, we can best do so through Jesus. We should follow him (Matthew 4:19 and Luke 14:27), believe in him (John 6:35), and be his disciples (John 8:31 and John 15:8).

These are all ways of saying we need to go all in for Jesus. That's it.

That's our essential doctrine. Everything else is secondary. Beyond Jesus and love, we shouldn't argue about the rest. We are to be one church, just as Jesus prayed we would be (John 17:20–21).

Yet in the last 500 years we've argued about doctrine, we've judged others by our religious perspectives, and we've killed people for their beliefs. We deemed that our view was right and everyone else was wrong. We used this to divide ourselves. We formed groups of like-minded thinkers, which became denominations. Today we have 42,000 Protestant denominations, dividing Jesus's church so much that we've lost our witness to the world. Jesus wanted his followers to live in unity. Yet we persist in division. The denominations that we've made are the antithesis of God's unity that Jesus wants (Ephesians 4:3–6).

Yes, division occurred in the first millennia and a half of Jesus's church—but that was nothing compared to what's happened in the last five centuries during the modern era.

Paul says that we are to unite ourselves under Jesus, to be like-minded, of one Spirit and one mind. In our relationships we should have Jesus's mindset (Philippians 2:1–5). In the book of Titus, Paul writes that we should warn a divisive person one time, and give a second notice if they disregard the first. Then the only recourse is to ignore them (Titus 3:10–11). Jude also warns against division. Instead of taking sides, he tells us to rise above it by focusing on growing our faith, praying in the Holy Spirit, and abiding in God's love (Jude 1:18–23).

Make Disciples, Not Converts

Jesus wants us to be his disciples. Each of the biographies of Jesus mention this. To be his disciple means to set all else aside and follow him (Matthew 16:24, Mark 8:34, Luke 9:23, and Luke 14:26–33). As his disciples, he expects us to produce fruit, that is to help other people become disciples too (John 15:8).

Matthew's biography of Jesus records his final instructions to his disciples before he returns to heaven. Jesus tells his followers to go everywhere and make disciples (Matthew 28:18–20). He doesn't say he wants them to go and make converts. Though believing in God is the first step, it's not enough. Jesus wants disciples. He wants followers who go all in for him.

Much of today's church has missed this call for discipleship. Instead, they focus on conversions, such as praying a prayer, being baptized, or making a public declaration of belief in Jesus. But this is just the first step on a lifelong journey of faith, a journey into discipleship.

Jesus commands us to make disciples, yet few churches do. And few people do.

When a person says "yes" to Jesus, that's wonderful news and the angels celebrate (Luke 15:10). Yet too many churches then abandon those new believers and leave them to flounder (Luke 8:11–15). Instead, they should invest in that person and help them become a disciple of Jesus, just as he commanded.

Kingdom of God

What if Jesus never intended us to form a church?

Let's look at where the Bible talks about the kingdom of God/kingdom of heaven and where it talks about church. (Mark and Luke refer to the *kingdom of God*, whereas Matthew prefers *kingdom of heaven*. The phrases are synonymous.)

Kingdom of God, kingdom of Heaven, and *church* are New Testament concepts. These terms don't occur anywhere in the Old Testament. Jesus talks much about the kingdom of God/heaven (eighty-five times) and little about church (three times, and then only in Matthew). Clearly Jesus focuses his teaching on the kingdom of God. Since Jesus comes to fulfill the Law (Matthew 5:17), the kingdom of God must be how he intends to do so. If the kingdom of God is so important to Jesus, it should be important to us. After all,

Jesus did tell his followers to "seek first the kingdom of God" (Matthew 6:33 ESV).

Today's church should push aside her traditions and practices to replace them with what Jesus teaches about the kingdom of God. Jesus explains the kingdom of God through parables:

- The parable of the weeds (Matthew 13:24–30)
- The parable of scattering seed (Mark 4:26–29)
- The parable of the mustard seed (Matthew 13:31–32, Mark 4:31–32, and Luke 13:18–19)
- The parable of yeast (Matthew 13:33 and Luke 13:20–21)
- The parable of the hidden treasure (Matthew 13:44)
- The parable of the pearl (Matthew 13:45–46)
- The parable of the net (Matthew 13:47–50)
- The parable of settling accounts (Matthew 18:23–35 and Matthew 25:14–30)
- The parable of the workers in the vineyard (Matthew 20:1–16)
- The parable of the wedding banquet (Matthew 22:2–14)
- The parable of the ten virgins (Matthew 25:1–13)

We should use these parables to inform our view of God and grow our relationship with him and others.

In addition, when Jesus talks about the kingdom of God, he mentions how close it is, saying that it's near (Luke 10:9). It's within his disciples' lifetimes (Mark 9:1), even present (Luke 17:21). How do we understand this immediacy of the kingdom of God? Isn't *kingdom of God* a synonym for heaven? Doesn't it mean eternal life? If so, how could it have been near 2,000 years ago but not here now, becoming an outcome we anticipate in our future?

Though an aspect of the kingdom of God looks forward to our eternity with Jesus in heaven, there's more to it. We must view the kingdom of God as both a present reality *and* a future promise.

Yes, the kingdom of God is about our hope for heaven when we die, but it's also about our time on earth now. The kingdom of God is about Jesus and his salvation, along with the life we lead in response to his gift to us. The kingdom of God is about eternal life, *and* that eternal life begins today. Heaven is just phase two. We're living in phase one—at least we should be. We'll do well to embrace Jesus's teaching about the kingdom of God as to how we should act today.

Jesus taught about the kingdom of God, but we made a church instead.

We must reform our ideas of our church practices to reshape them from a biblical perspective. Here are the nine actions we discussed:

1. *Dismiss the importance we put on our church buildings and replace it with a people-first perspective.*

2. *Stop paying people to do what the Bible calls us to do ourselves as priests who serve one another.*

3. *Reform our perspective on money, realizing that 100 percent belongs to God. We are merely stewards of it, and we must use it wisely for the greatest kingdom impact.*

4. *Remove membership, which segregates people, and instead embrace Jesus's perspective of inclusion.*

5. *Stop insisting on man-made credentials for our ministers and consider godly character instead.*

6. *Tell our children about Jesus and not expect Sunday school to do our job, allowing us to reclaim that time as a community service opportunity.*

7. *Pursue unity in Jesus and oppose every instance of division.*

8. *Go and make disciples as Jesus commanded.*

9. *Think more about the kingdom of God and less about church.*

Questions: Which of these perspectives convicts you the most? What steps can you take to change how you act to better align with what the Bible says and what Jesus did?

Chapter 10:

Next Steps

Congratulations on making it this far in the book. You can play a significant role in the future of Jesus's church—if you choose to. But whether you remain mired in the past or shift into the future is up to you and how you react. There are three ways you can respond. No, four.

Do Nothing

You may have found this book interesting, even a bit thought-provoking—at least from an intellectual standpoint. But you'll lay it down and not give it much more thought. The ideas will fade from memory, and soon they'll disappear. Nothing will change. You won't change.

You will persist with your embrace of status quo Christianity. That's easy to do. That's the safe response. If you want easy and safe, your journey ends now. Thank you for giving this book your consideration.

But I hope this isn't you. If you need more time to contemplate this radical departure from what you're used to, please ease on into the next section.

Think About It

This book may have ignited something deep in your soul. You've always known something wasn't quite right with your church experiences, hoping that each new Sunday destination would produce a fresh outcome. But in the end, it was just more of the same.

You might suspect this book has provided the answers you seek or at least pointed you in the right direction. You pledge to think about it. Contemplating the prescriptions in this book is a good start, a great beginning. But thinking is not doing.

You find yourself at a crossroads. Do nothing more than consider this book and you'll easily slide back into the first category, the do-nothing readers.

To shift from neutral to drive, share this book with someone you think might be hungry for its message. Or tap a friend if you sense that they align with your unspoken angst about today's church practices. Together, encourage one another to drive forward, accelerating headlong into your future, just as iron sharpens iron (Proverbs 27:17). Better yet, find two like-minded friends to journey down this path with you. With the three of you working together you're more likely to succeed. Remember, a three-stranded rope is much stronger (Ecclesiastes 4:12).

As you discuss these concepts and move ahead, you and your friends will leave mere thinking behind to embrace tangible, life-changing, kingdom-advancing action. Read on to nudge your thoughts into movement that will help you surge forward and embrace one of the next two responses, be it to pursue incremental change or to embrace total transformation.

Pursue Incremental Change

If you're on staff at a church, especially in a paid ministry position, this book represents a danger to your career which could threaten to derail your financial future. If you're successful in following this advice in full, you'll work yourself out of a job. That's a terrifying outcome. You may have a family to support, a mortgage to pay, and scarcely enough funds to make it through the month. You need this job and can't put it at risk. You won't.

Yet stopping short of a complete overhaul, you do see where you can make smaller yet meaningful changes, operating on your church with surgical precision to produce a healthier patient. You feel a call to pursue incremental change.

Or you may be part of the laity. You attend one of today's churches and enjoy it. You don't want to abandon what you know and love. You just want to see a few strategic tweaks to get it back on track, a path a bit better aligned with Scripture. You feel a pull to streamline and simplify your church infrastructure. You question if your facility needs another addition or wonder how necessary that new paid staff position really is. You may shake your head as you study your church budget, wondering if God is pleased at how much money goes to maintain your church and how little goes to help others and advance his kingdom.

You feel the Holy Spirit's prompting to be a catalyst for change. You want to be an advocate for incremental improvement. If you're not in leadership, tread carefully. Proceed in prayer and under Holy Spirit power. Even if you do, your friends at church could still label you a troublemaker and push you aside or force you out.

Regardless of whether you serve in a leadership position and can promote reform or reside in the laity and desire to advocate change, here are a few incremental improvements to consider:

Eliminate Membership: God wasn't pleased with David counting his army. It caused the king to put his confidence in his troops and not the Almighty (2 Samuel 24). So, too, in addition to dividing the body of Christ into two groups, counting members can result in us taking pride in our numbers and not in our God.

Yes, people in our churches want to know membership tallies, and even more so our denominations, yet there is no biblical benefit or mandate to do so. Therefore, stop promoting membership.

Ditch Your Denomination: Since we're talking about denominations, they are another source of division, sowing disunity among Jesus's church. Leave your denomination. But don't go in the huff, creating hard feelings. Exit peacefully (Romans 12:18). This may be a big ask, but don't dismiss it just because it feels too extreme. Pray about it. Ask God for direction (James 1:5).

Deemphasize Sunday Meetings: Instead of one large gathering on Sunday morning, promote smaller distributed meetings in homes. These can occur on Sundays or anytime throughout the week. The principles of the small group movement are a place to start, but small groups are not the goal. House church principles provide even more ideas for these small, at-home gatherings. To learn more, there are scores of insightful books and resources about both small groups and house churches.

Equip Priests: Remember that God wanted his children to be a nation of priests and Jesus died to make it so. Now we need to start acting like it. This requires us reprogramming what we've learned and what we've experienced. We must stop expecting our paid clergy to minister to us and instead minister to one another as priests, just as the Bible prescribes.

Celebrate Community: We need to deemphasize the focus of our church services on song and sermon to reemphasize the importance of spiritual community. This is sharing life with one another and enjoying meals. It's encouraging one another and serving each other. It's about supporting one another as preparation to minister to those in our neighborhoods.

Re-envision Sunday School: Remind parents that their job is to educate their children about Jesus. Yes, they can tap into other resources and programs to do this, but let's remove Sunday school from its all-too-important pedestal as a Christian education tool.

Let's re-envision Sunday school as a resource to serve unmet needs in your community.

Teach Service: Jesus lived a life that modeled service to others, of helping the people he encountered. He didn't expect others to serve him. He came to serve them (Mark 10:45). We should do the same.

Emphasize the "One Another" Commands: In chapter 5 we listed all the biblical instructions for how we should treat one another. Now we need to obey these commands and put them into practice. Our Christian community will be better for it. And this will empower our witness to a watching world when they see our faith put into action by how well we treat others.

Fix the Budget: From a spiritual perspective, let me assert that our church budgets are broken. They're misaligned. We must fix them. This means spending less money on our church's internal needs and more on kingdom activity. This means we should help other Jesus followers who struggle in need and tell our neighbors about Jesus's good news.

Yes, money is a divisive topic, but God's call to spend our funds wisely isn't. This brings us to stewardship.

Emphasize Stewardship: From a legalistic, Old Testament perspective we may conclude that 10 percent of our income belongs to God, which implies the other 90 percent is ours to do with as we please. False.

God blesses us financially and expects that we will spend his provisions with care. We are to bless others (Genesis 12:1–3). We are to function as wise stewards to administer the funds he has blessed us with, whether much or little (Matthew 25:14–30). Self-indulgent spending, extravagant lifestyles, and ill-advised purchases do not honor God or advance his kingdom. This must stop.

Remember, however, that astute stewardship does not equate to funding a local church. It may. Or God may call you to use the money he has blessed you with for an even greater purpose. Think, pray, and listen before you give.

Return Communion to Homes: Most churches celebrate communion regularly, be it each Sunday, once a month, or quarterly. This ceremony provides meaning for some and bores others.

Remember, however, that communion is Jesus's extension of the Passover meal, which was an annual celebration that took place in people's homes with their families and neighbors. We should empower the laity to reclaim communion, reforming it from church ritual and returning it to our homes where it started—and belongs.

Promote Christian Unity: Jesus wants his followers to be one, to function in complete harmony. We must stop dividing his one church into theological factions and arguing armies focused on trivialities at the expense of believing in Jesus, following him, and being his disciples—as one body, the body of Christ (1 Corinthians 12:12–27).

Act Now: Pick one of these items and work to reform it. Then move on to another. Go through this list and you'll revitalize your church. Yes, you'll lose some status-quo attendees and change-adverse detractors along the way, but these people aren't the future of Jesus's church. They are part of its broken past, a past we must leave behind forever.

Embrace Total Transformation

Working within the system to make incremental change is one strategy. It may, however, prove to be an ongoing struggle to promote needed reforms and persist in their pursuit. This is because of those who are content to have church practices remain the same. They cling to what they grew up with, what they like, and what makes them comfortable.

Another option, one that borders on revolution, is a total overhaul of what *is* to produce a new outcome of what *should be*. This means replacing what is with something new. This means walking away from your church.

When you go down this path, don't stir up dissension within the congregation you're leaving. Don't seek to take as many people with you as you can. Instead, leave quietly, even stealthily.

Start Small: As you begin your new adventure of pursuing the kingdom of God in a biblical way, think small (Zechariah 4:10). This could be as simple as inviting a friend to have coffee with you once a week. This doesn't need to be an overtly spiritual time or an intentionally sacred meeting. The one essential is that you gather in Jesus's name. Then he will join with you (Matthew 18:20). This is your new church. Welcome it as the beginning of your new spiritual community.

Stay Small: Church-growth experts may seize on this small beginning, encouraging a numerical increase to where it morphs into a house church. They'll later advocate that it organizes into one of today's churches, complete with building, paid staff, and financial needs just like in the Bible—the Old Testament of the Bible, that is, not the New. But they'll do this at the expense of Jesus's fulfillment of the Old Testament Law and prophets.

You can certainly invite others to join you, but keep the roster small. Encourage everyone to participate in whatever form your get-togethers take (1 Corinthians 14:26). Follow the leading of the Holy Spirit (Acts 13:2 and Galatians 5:16–18).

As you meet, be sure to keep your focus on Jesus and his Holy Spirit. They will guide you in ways to look beyond your group, to be missional (Matthew 10:42). Groups with an internal focus, selfishly fixated on themselves, usually fizzle out after a year or two. Groups with an external focus are more apt to persist for the long term.

Let God guide you into this. It might be working together at a homeless shelter, volunteering at the food pantry, or tutoring students who need a bit of extra help. As you do so, proceed in Jesus's name (Mark 9:41).

Make Money Matter: It should take no money for your group to function. And if your get-togethers carry an expense, let each person pay their own way. You don't need to take an offering, and you certainly don't need a budget.

Instead, encourage each person to give money to the causes the Holy Spirit prompts them to support. Think of individual needs and small, lean ministries, not institutions.

Replicate: As we've already mentioned, the goal is not to grow your group, to scale into something large. Instead, model community and help other groups form. This distributed model of church is far different from our centralized, large-group Sunday meetings that we experience today. But it seems more aligned with the grassroots example of the early church in the Bible.

Shared Leadership: There's a danger when functioning in isolation. This is especially concerning if one dynamic individual leads your group. Instead, promote mutual leadership, with each person leading as appropriate, ministering to one another in an egalitarian manner. This is a key strategy to escape going down the wrong path and avoid a slide into heresy that can happen from following the unexamined teachings of one persuasive leader.

Network: Beyond having mutual leadership within your group, network with other like-minded groups to encourage each other to function as Jesus's church. This provides accountability and support.

Celebrate: You may want to have your groups get together occasionally to have a larger, shared celebration of what God is doing *in* and *through* your groups to advance his kingdom. But think of a picnic or a retreat, not a church service. In doing so, avoid having this become a regular Sunday event. Otherwise you risk reinstating the Old Testament model of church you're attempting to leave behind.

Remember, God's people in the Old Testament did not meet every Sabbath. Their command was to keep the seventh day holy and not do any work. Yes, some of their annual celebrations did fall on the Sabbath, and they did gather on those days. But it wasn't a weekly occurrence. It was a special event, a special time to come together in celebration.

The choice is yours. You can set this book aside and settle for what is. Or you can inhale deeply and step forward in faith, trusting Jesus and following the Holy Spirit as you do your part to fix Jesus's broken church.

Pray for guidance on what to do next. Write it down to keep your God-given vision on track. Then go and do it.

Questions: Which of these four categories do you best fit into? What can you do today to move forward? Who should you invite to journey with you?

Moving Forward

I would like to tell you that I gather weekly in a non-church setting with other like-minded followers of Jesus. We meet to share what God is doing in our lives, teach one another, and encourage each other to move forward in our faith practices. In between our meetings we hang out in restaurants, coffee shops, and homes, experiencing vibrant Christian community. We also go out to serve others in Jesus's name, encourage people in their faith journey, and point spiritual seekers to God.

I want to tell you all this, but I can't. I'm not there yet, at least not in totality.

Over the years I've done many things to move toward a meaningful Christian community that more closely follows the New Testament narrative and aligns with what Jesus accomplished when he fulfilled the Old Testament Law and prophets.

Here are some of the things I do or have done to realize this:

- Regularly gather with others in a restaurant or home to share a meal and celebrate Jesus
- Help feed the hungry
- Teach budget classes and encourage those who struggle with their finances
- Transform a church-based small group into an independent community group
- Meet weekly in a coffee shop to mentor new believers and struggling Christians
- Celebrate communion at home with family and in restaurants with friends
- Gather to offer prayer and healing to those in need
- Attend a house church to encourage people on their faith journey, regardless of their background, doctrine, or situation
- Do street ministry to interact with spiritual seekers and church dropouts, offering encouragement, prayer, and love
- Conduct services at a homeless shelter
- Meet to study Scripture and then practice what we've learned

Together, these actions have moved me into a closer relationship with Jesus and enabled me to experience a more holistic and meaningful spiritual community, which had never happened before in a structured church setting.

Most of the people who have journeyed with me in these various initiatives have done so while maintaining a connection to one of today's churches. Only a few have embraced these moves as their only church experience and their sole spiritual community, which is the preferred goal.

I've also learned that as people interact in more intimate spiritual community, things often get messy. The challenge is to embrace the messiness as a normal part of true community and not run from it. The easy response, however, is to retreat to what we've always done and what we know, to go to church on Sunday where it's comfortable and we can avoid the messier parts of life.

In this book, I've opened a door to a new possibility, which celebrates an old practice. As we move into this, may my ceiling be your floor.

Whether you pursue the vision painted in the first paragraph of this chapter or take incremental steps, such as the ones I listed, the point is to move forward to more fully embrace what Jesus calls us to and resist staying mired in status-quo Christianity.

Questions: Which of these possibilities most connects with you? What other ideas do you have? Are you ready to move forward to better realize all that Jesus has in mind for you and his church? What roadblocks do you need God's help in overcoming?

Further Discussion

J esus's *Broken Church* makes an ideal discussion
guide for your family and friends. In preparation for the conversation, read one of this book's
chapters and then meet to discuss it.

- Start by praying and asking for Holy Spirit insight and clarity.
- Focus on the discussion questions at the end
  of each chapter. In addition, consider the ital-
  icized thought that precedes the questions.
- Discuss other elements of the section as needed.
- End by asking God to help you put into action what you've learned.

After you've worked through all the chapters,
wrap up by deciding how to proceed. Then move forward in Holy Spirit power, just like Jesus's church did
in the Bible (Acts 1:4–5).

Acknowledgments

It seems God has used my whole life to prepare me to research and contemplate what to put in this book. For that I thank and praise him.

Along the way he's brought others into my life to guide me in this journey. I won't share names, because I'll surely forget someone, and I don't want to do that. Besides, you know who you are. And if you're asking yourself, "Might he mean me?", the answer is "Yes!" Thank you for helping bring me to this point in my spiritual journey.

Last, I acknowledge all who read this book. May God use my words to move you from status quo Christianity to life-changing revolution—for his honor and glory.

About Peter DeHaan

Peter DeHaan, PhD wants to change the world one word at a time. His books and blog posts discuss God, the Bible, and church, geared toward spiritual seekers and church dropouts. Many people feel church has let them down, and Peter seeks to encourage them as they search for a place to belong.

But he's not afraid to ask tough questions or make religious people squirm. He's not trying to be provocative, but he seeks truth, even if it makes some people uncomfortable. Peter urges Christians to push past the status quo and reexamine how they practice their faith in every area of their lives.

Peter DeHaan earned his doctorate, awarded with high distinction, from Trinity College of the Bible and Theological Seminary. He lives with his wife in beautiful Southwest Michigan and wrangles crossword puzzles in his spare time.

A lifelong student of the Bible, Peter wrote the 700-page website ABibleADay.com to encourage people to explore the Bible, the greatest book ever written. His popular blog, at PeterDeHaan.com, addresses biblical spirituality to build a faith that matters.

Connect with him and learn more at PeterDeHaan.com.

If you liked *Jesus's Broken Church,* please leave a review online. Your review will help other people discover this book and encourage them to read it too. That would be amazing.

Thank you.

Books by Peter DeHaan

For a complete, up-to-date list of all Peter's books, go to PeterDeHaan.com/books.

Dear Theophilus series:

- *Dear Theophilus: A 40-Day Devotional Exploring the Life of Jesus through the Gospel of Luke*

- *Dear Theophilus Acts: 40 Devotional Insights for Today's Church*

- *Dear Theophilus Isaiah: 40 Prophetic Insights about Jesus, Justice, and Gentiles*

- *Dear Theophilus Minor Prophets: 40 Prophetic Teachings about Unfaithfulness, Punishment, and Hope*

- *Dear Theophilus Job: 40 Insights About Moving from Despair to Deliverance*

- *Dear Theophilus John's Gospel: 40 Reflections about Jesus's Life and Love*

52 Churches series:

- *52 Churches: A Yearlong Journey Encountering God, His Church, and Our Common Faith*

- *The 52 Churches Workbook: Become a Church that Matters*

- *More Than 52 Churches: The Journey Continues*

- *The More Than 52 Churches Workbook: Pursue Christian Community and Grow in Our Faith*

Bible Bios series:

- *Women of the Bible: The Victorious, the Victims, the Virtuous, and the Vicious*

- *Friends and Foes of Jesus: Explore How People in the New Testament React to God's Good News*

Other books:

- *Woodpecker Wars: Celebrating the Spirituality of Everyday Life*

- *95 Tweets: Celebrating Martin Luther in the 21st Century*

- *How Big is Your Tent? A Call for Christian Unity, Tolerance, and Love*

Be the first to hear about Peter's new books and receive updates when you sign up at www.PeterDeHaan. com/updates.

Printed in Great Britain
by Amazon